CHRISTIAN HEALING

CHRISTIAN HEALING

Stepping into Your Authority and God's Anointing to Heal the Sick

ANTHONY SCOTT INGRAM

Anthony Scott Ingram

www.AnthonyIngram.com

First Printing, 2021

Dedicated to all those who are desperate for a faith that is real.

CONTENTS

INTRODUCTION

I love the healing ministry. After a year living in Haiti in 2012, where I was called on to pray for the sick regularly, healing has been one of my biggest pursuits among the things of God. Then, after an impartation prayer by Dr. Randy Clark (Global Awakening[1]) in which healing was activated mightily in October of that same year, healing prayer has become a vital part of my global ministry. I have seen the power of God to heal on thousands of occasions, in my own body, through my prayers for others, and through the many believers I have been privileged to equip in praying for the sick. (You can read all about my journey into the healing ministry in the Appendix.)

Due to years of deep bible study and an incredible amount of personal experience in the area of healing, for me, this is no longer a topic of theological debate. To say that God still heals today is a foregone conclusion in my mind and is therefore not a controversy I feel the need to engage in. I am not writing this book to argue a point or prove anyone wrong. My mind is settled. I will leave it to more intellectual, "professional" theologians to debate. I will simply tell you "what I have seen and heard" and then keep laying hands on the sick and watching them recover, the way I have for nearly a decade.

The release of this book comes at a strategic time, as the world is coming out from under the oppression of a major global pandemic called COVID19. As this sickness has wrecked the world's stability in so many ways, I feel there is a great need to stir up the children of God to understand their healing inheritance in Jesus Christ. I also feel a strong conviction in my spirit that another major healing revival, like that of the mid-1900s, is coming very soon.[2] There is, therefore, a great need for believers to learn to practice the gift of healing given by the Holy Spirit. That is the purpose behind this writing.

I ask that you don't just take my word as truth. I highly encourage you to study the scriptures for yourself while asking the Holy Spirit to guide you into truth. My desire is that this book would be a starting point, not a finish line, in your journey into healing. I aim to lay the biblical foundations for God's healing work, give you the confidence to trust that God still heals today, and show you how you can take part in this ministry yourself.

Finally, as you read, I want you to know that I am writing as a pastor and fellow minister, not as a Bible scholar. What I share will have a lot of biblical truth and scriptural support, but the purpose of this writing is to be practical, not just theoretical. I desire that at the end of this reading, you will be bold enough to take a risk of faith, lay hands on the sick, and see what God will do.

God bless you in this journey.
Anthony Scott Ingram
June 2021

Endnotes

[1] www.GlobalAwakening.com

[2] I shared the word God spoke to me on my blog, here: http://anthonyingram.com/another-healing-revival-is-coming/

| 1 |

The Biblical Basis for Healing

*Bless the LORD, O my soul, and forget not all his benefits, who forgives all your iniquity, **who heals all your diseases**, who redeems your life from the pit, who crowns you with steadfast love and mercy, who satisfies you with good so that your youth is renewed like the eagle's. - Psalm 103:2-5 (emphasis mine)*

The Theological Divide

Throughout the history of the church, there have been many points of division between believers and theologians in different streams of the Christian faith. One of those divisions has been over the extent of God's promise to heal the sick. As the church moved from the New Testament age, through the time of the early church fathers, differing opinions began to form about the extent of God's healing; about who should even be allowed to practice this gift, or if we should even expect healing to happen at all, on this side of eternity.

As we begin to look at the biblical foundations for healing, we must seek to overcome divisions formed from man's opinions and look at the whole of scripture alone. The major problem is that the bible itself places God's divine healing of human sicknesses in tension between the "already but not yet" reality of the Kingdom of God. This is the idea that when Jesus was on earth, He initiated God's Kingdom with all its gifts and promises now (the already), and yet there is still more to come in the final consummation of all things at His second coming (the not yet).

This tension has all too often created a major point of division between believers who hold differing views of this gift. Some argue that God's promise of healing was only for the early days of the church, or "the apostolic age.' This was to prove that Jesus Christ was the Messiah and then to give credibility to the establishment of the church. According to this view, now that the church's witness has spread all over the world and we have the complete canon of scriptures in the Bible, those gifts have ceased. This viewpoint is called cessationism.

Among cessationists, some believe that, although the gifts are not necessary for "the church age," they will be re-established at some point before Christ's return to usher in the last days. However, most cessationists believe that the promise of healing cannot be claimed for now. We must wait for these things to come in eternity or possibly in a future millennial kingdom when "*He will wipe away every tear from their eyes, and death shall be no more, neither shall there be mourning, nor crying, nor pain anymore, for the former things have passed away.*"[1]

Although cessationism has had its stronghold in the church, especially in Western Christianity, since the Protestant Reformation, today, the majority of Christians in the world believe that healing has continued up to the present day. They claim not only biblical evidence but also contemporary testimonies to prove their case. This view is called continuationism and seems to be the most widespread viewpoint of global Christians. This is also the opinion held by myself and the ministry I oversee.[2]

As each theological point of view takes shape, the people on every side begin to make theological arguments to prove that God's healing gift only exists within the time period their position claims. The problem with taking sides and arguing about "when" God heals (or doesn't) is that the Bible itself refuses to limit God's healing to any set period of time. Past, present, or future, the answer, biblically is "yes," and both the scriptures and historical evidence prove this point.[3]

"Yes," God granted major healing in the apostolic age;

"Yes," God wrought many major healing miracles in the first few centuries of the church;

"Yes," God continues to do many great healing miracles now through the faith of His people, and

"Yes," God will heal everyone completely at His second coming.

As we begin to lay the foundation for Chrisitan healing throughout human history, we must go back to the beginning of God's redemptive work in humanity to understand His promise to heal.

Jehovah Rapha

From the beginning of God's personal revelation of himself to the people of Israel, He has declared Himself to be Jehovah Rapha, meaning "I AM Healer" or "YHWH, Your Healer." He makes this revelation in Exodus 15:26, immediately following the crossing of the Red Sea.

> *"If you will diligently listen to the voice of the LORD your God, and do that which is right in his eyes, and give ear to his commandments and keep all His statutes, I will put none of the diseases on you that I put on the Egyptians, for* ***I am the LORD, your healer****."*

The Hebrew word "Rapha" and its derivatives mean "heal, cure, and restore." It is used 86 times throughout the Old Testament and is commonly used to describe God's restorative work in Israel throughout the Old Testament.

Sometimes it is used directly for God healing people from disease and afflictions, such as Genesis 20:17,

> *"Then Abraham prayed to God, and God* ***healed*** *Abimelech, and also* ***healed*** *his wife and female slaves so that they bore children."*

Sometimes the word "Rapha" is used in a larger sense of the rebuilding of the nation and cities at various points in their history, such as is promised in 2 Chronicled 7:14,

> *"if my people who are called by my name humble themselves, and pray and seek my face and turn from their wicked ways, then*

*I will hear from heaven and will forgive their sin and **heal** their land."*

Although space will not allow me to give a complete overview of God's restorative practices in the Old Testament and the surrounding requirements which are often attached (repentance, humility, etc.), the point I want us to grasp is that from the beginning, God has revealed Himself as Healer. It is one of His divine names. It is part of His identity. Undeniably, then, part of God's nature is to heal and restore both the people caught in sickness and His broken creation.

History has proven that God is not waiting for the future to start healing. He has already been doing so throughout the world, in every generation, and we know that He does not change! He is the same yesterday, today, and forever" (See Malachi 3:6 and Hebrews 13:8).

If God has revealed Himself as Jehovah Rapha, then to disbelieve that He will heal His people is to break the Third Commandment given to Moses: *"You shall not take the name of the Lord your God in vain..."* To do so is to hear His revealed name — God Your Healer — and yet empty it of its power and therefore sin by our disbelief.

Healing in the Messiah

Throughout the Old Testament, God makes many promises to His people, Israel. Among them are redemption, salvation, protection, provision, restoration, and healing. As the Old Testament moves from the Exodus and settling in the promised land into the period of the Kings and Prophets, many of these promises become aligned, not just with YHWH, Himself, but with a mysterious "Anointed One" or "Messiah" who would come.

From Genesis 3:15 onward, God's promise of a Savior begins to take shape. He would be a child of Abraham[4], in the line of King David[5], but would also be called *"Wonderful Counselor, Mighty God, Everlasting Father and Prince of Peace."[6]* The growing expectation of the Old Testament is that this Messiah would both fully reveal and fully accomplish all of God's redemptive plans on earth!

Not only would this coming Messiah bring the forgiveness of sins, but He would also pay the price to earn our healing[7]. We see this in the prophetic revelation God gives concerning the Messiah and in the expectation of those people who walked in relationship with God throughout the ages. Again, due to space, I will simply give two examples of this here, although many more could be listed:

The Prophetic Revelation from God

In Isaiah 53, we get what is considered by many to be the clearest picture of the gospel in the Old Testament. Though I would encourage you to read the entire passage, I will simply share verse 5 for our purposes here:

> *"But he was pierced for our transgressions; he was crushed for our iniquities; upon him was the chastisement that brought us peace, and with his wounds we are healed."*

Although many people try to spiritualize this as a metaphor for our brokenness and sinful nature, we will see shortly that this is not how the New Testament writers interpreted it.

The Expectation of God's Human Friends

Not only did the prophets prophesy that healing would be in the atonement of Christ, but the expectation of those who knew God personally viewed God's promise of the healing of sickness and disease to be equal with His promise to forgive sin!

As King David writes in Psalm 103:2-3:

> *"Bless the LORD, O my soul, and forget not all his benefits,* ***who forgives all your iniquity, who heals all your diseases****..."*

From the most basic reading of the Old Testament prophecies, it is evident that healing would be an essential part of the atonement of the Messiah because as sin is dealt with, so are its effects. Thus, the Messiah would bring about God's promise of healing, just as He would fulfill God's promise to establish a Kingdom and restore the creation!

Jesus Claims to Be the Fulfillment of God's Messianic Promises

As we move from the Old Testament into the New Testament, we meet Jesus. Over and over again, the goal of the gospel writers is to show us that Jesus is the Messiah who was promised. One of the main proofs they offer is that Jesus healed the sick!

As Jesus gets ready to begin His public ministry at age 30, He is baptized and then goes into the wilderness to fast and pray and be tempted by the devil. When He returns from the wilderness, we see His first public ministry appearance. In Luke 4:16-21, Jesus stands in the synagogue in Nazareth and declares Himself to be the long-anticipated Messiah! He read from the prophet Isaiah, where it says,

> *"The Spirit of the Lord is upon me, because he has anointed me to proclaim good news to the poor. He has sent me to proclaim liberty to the captives and recovering of sight to the blind, to set at liberty those who are oppressed, to proclaim the year of the Lord's favor."*

Then, as He finished and people were waiting for Him to teach on the passage, He simply said, *"Today this Scripture has been fulfilled in your hearing."*

This was a bold move by Jesus, and it almost got Him killed. However, if we are to take Him at His word, we must look at what He said. After all, this was His self-introduction as Messiah to the world.

Included in this fulfillment declaration of Isaiah was the promise of healing, pictured in this passage as *"the recovering of sight to the blind."* (This again is something some modern scholars try to spiritualize as being blind in our sin, yet the New Testament points to Jesus' healing of blind eyes repeatedly as validation of His Messiahship.)

The Healing Ministry of Jesus

As we read through the gospels, it is safe to say that Jesus' healing ministry cannot be contained in a couple of short paragraphs. It spanned the entirety of His earthly ministry, and the gospel writers share many stories of physical healing. However, to give one highlight of His healing practice, in Matthew 8:16-17, we read this:

> *"That evening they brought to him many who were oppressed by demons, and he cast out the spirits with a word* ***and healed all who were sick****. This was to fulfill what was spoken by the prophet Isaiah: 'He took our illnesses and bore our diseases.'"*

In truth, as you read the gospels, it seems that Jesus, in His earthly ministry, never left a sick person unhealed. He never prayed, "God, if it is Your will, heal this person." Instead, He took the promise of Isaiah 53 as a literal promise that He would have authority over all sicknesses, so he healed everyone who came to Him.

Exactly as the Old Testament prophesied and hoped that the Messiah would bring healing, Jesus became the fulfillment of that promise. While He was on earth, Jesus did not simply promise healing at the consummation of His Kingdom. He brought healing immediately!

From the beginning of God's self-revelation as Jehovah Rapha to Jesus' revelation as Emmanuel — the Messiah — God has declared and proven Himself to be a healing God in the *present tense.* Physical healing was expected to be in the atonement of the Messiah, and Jesus proved the expectation to be true!

It is upon this foundation that we must begin to put our faith in who Jesus says He is and who He has proven Himself to be over and over again.

There is a biblical basis (not just anecdotal) to believe that healing is not limited to the second coming of Jesus. However, there is still the issue of how healing would be carried on, from Jesus' earthly ministry to the modern-day, and there are some objections we must face if we are to claim that Jesus is still healing.

Endnotes

[1] Revelation 21:4

[2] www.SozoMinistries.net

[3] While a full history of Biblical healing and its continuation throughout history is impossible to share in this short book; I would highly recommend a couple of other books on the subject: The first is "2000 Years of Charismatic Christianity" by Eddie L. Hyatt. This book is not centralized on healing but shows how all the gifts of the Holy Spirit have been around continually since Jesus' departure. The second is "Regeneration: A Complete History of Healing in the Christian Church" by J.D. King. This three-volume set is the most thorough handling of the topic I

have found, including that volume 3 is nothing more than a 400-page bibliography!

[4] Prophesied in Genesis 12:3. Fulfilled in Jesus according to Acts 3:24–26

[5] Prophesied in 2 Samuel 7:12–16; Isaiah 11:1; Jeremiah 23:5–6. Fulfilled in Jesus according to Matthew 1:1; Luke 1:32–33; Acts 15:15–16; Hebrews 1:5

[6] Prophesied in Isaiah 9:6–7. Fulfilled in Jesus according to Matthew 12:42; Luke 1:32–33, 79; John 14:27; Acts 10:36; Romans 9:5; Colossians 2:3; 2 Thessalonians 3:3

[7] Prophesied in Isaiah 53:5. Fulfilled by Jesus according to 1 Peter 2:24.

| 2 |

Is Healing For Today?

In the last chapter, we laid out the biblical foundation of Christian healing from God's revelation of Himself as Jehovah Rapha to the fulfillment of Messianic prophecy for healing in Jesus.

Now, I obviously believe that Jesus' healing gift was to carry on after His ascension to heaven, rather than to be relegated only to the future consummation of His Kingdom. Still, for the purpose of this writing, we are left with the challenge of proving biblically that it was Jesus' intention for healing to continue throughout the church age, up to today.

We finished the last chapter discussing that Jesus healed every sick person that was brought to Him. No one who believes in the Bible as God's Word disputes this fact. However, in answering the question of whether healing would continue today, we must face certain objections that are often raised against divine healing moving forward from the New Testament period.

Objection: Jesus Was God! We are Not!

One common objection to God's healing today is, "Jesus was God; of course He could heal everyone. We are not!" This objection, however, voluntarily overlooks the humanity of Jesus in the incarnation.

The bible clearly states that although Jesus is God in the flesh, He willingly laid His divine attributes aside and lived life as a human being.[1] Jesus was the perfect example of what humanity looks like when we are filled with the Holy Spirit and fully submitted to God. Theologically we call this "Christus Exemplar" or "Christ Our Example."

Jesus laid down His divine attributes; therefore, we must realize that Jesus was not healing people through His own power as God. Instead, he was healing people as a man who had been given authority by God and was anointed through the power of God the Holy Spirit. This is why the Bible does not record any healing on Jesus' part before the Holy Spirit descending on Him at His baptism. (We will discuss the difference between authority and anointing in the next chapter.)

The word "Messiah" means "Anointed One." Not only did Jesus heal through the power of the Holy Spirit's anointing, but he then promised the same Holy Spirit to His church. Through the Holy Spirit, our spiritual DNA is re-formed to be just like His, and we can operate in the same anointing that He did!

We see this in the fact that Jesus did not keep His authority to heal for Himself, but He commissioned His disciples to do the same thing. Matthew 10 tells us:

> *"And he called to him his twelve disciples and* ***gave them authority*** *over unclean spirits, to cast them out, and* ***to heal every disease and every affliction****... These twelve Jesus sent out, instructing them, "Go nowhere among the Gentiles and enter no town of the Samaritans, but go rather to the lost sheep of the house of Israel. And proclaim as you go, saying, 'The kingdom of heaven is at hand.'* ***Heal the sick, raise the dead, cleanse lepers****, cast out demons. You received without paying; give without pay."*[2]

Jesus not only thought it was possible for human beings to heal the sick, but He gave them the authority to do so and then commanded it!

Objection: That Gift Was Only for the 12 Apostles; Not Us!

The cessationist critic will argue that the supernatural gifts of the spirit were given only to those original 12 Apostles (or only for the Apostolic Age) to get Christianity started, but that the gifts did not continue past the death of the last Apostle.

Yet, again, however, scripture itself overturns this argument as Jesus did not limit the transfer of His authority only to the Apostles:

> ***"After this the Lord appointed seventy-two others*** *and sent them on ahead of him, two by two, into every town and place where he himself was about to go, and He said to them...Whenever you enter a town and they receive you, eat what is set before you.* ***Heal the***

> ***sick** in it and say to them, 'The kingdom of God has come near to you.'"*[3]

We clearly see Jesus Himself directing non-Apostles to heal the sick! And His healing ministry still doesn't end there.

Should We Expect Healing Today?

In His final charge to His disciples before leaving earth, He commissions them to instruct the next generation of disciples to continue in everything He had taught and commanded them!

> *"And Jesus came and said to them, 'All authority in heaven and on earth has been given to me. Go therefore and make disciples of all nations, baptizing them in the name of the Father and of the Son and of the Holy Spirit, teaching them to observe **all** that I have commanded you. And behold, I am with you always, to the end of the age.'"*[4]

I believe the "all" includes His command to heal the sick. In fact, in his presentation of this same "Great Commission," Mark's gospel says:

> *"And he said to them, 'Go into all the world and proclaim the gospel to the whole creation. Whoever believes and is baptized will be saved, but whoever does not believe will be condemned. And **these signs will accompany those who believe**: in my name they will cast out demons; they will speak in new tongues; they will pick up ser-*

> *pents with their hands; and if they drink any deadly poison, it will not hurt them;* ***they will lay their hands on the sick, and they will*** *recover."*[5]

The Great Commission, therefore, tells us that divine healing is intended to pass from one generation of believers to another. It would not stop! It seems the only caveat is that we must believe.

So, should we expect healing to continue today? YES! Not only is healing in the nature of God and the Atonement of Christ. It is also in the commission of the church!

I know many will still object to this fact by twisting minor verses in other places, but the truth is, you have to throw out a lot of scripture to conclude that Jesus does not heal today, through His church, and instead, to believe that He is withholding that gift until His final return.

Objection: Why Are Some People Not Healed?

Once we establish that healing is for today, biblically, critics will then turn their objections to secondary issues, such as *"Ok, well if God still heals, then why isn't everybody healed?"* This objection sometimes turns to personal attacks on those who believe in healing: *"Well, if you believe God heals, then why don't you go pray and shut down the hospitals?"* Other times, the objection is heartfelt: *"Well, if God heals, then why did my family member die of cancer, when so many people were praying for them?"*

The short answer is: I don't know. Biblically, you can point to many factors that might explain why some people do not get healed in prayer.

- It can be my lack of faith as a pray-er (James 5:15).
- It can be the person's lack of faith as the one being prayed for (Luke 8:48, 17:19, 18:42).
- It can be the existence of unconfessed sin.
- It can be the presence of demonic strongholds.
- It may even be a case of the sovereignty of God giving grace to the person, in which their sickness unto death spares them from a worse state (see Isaiah 57:1, with an example given in 1 Kings 14:12-13)

There are likely many other reasons people are not healed today. I don't know. I cannot give a definite answer as to why some people are healed now, supernaturally, and some are left in their state of sickness. All I can say for certain is that healing IS in the atonement of Jesus Christ and that whether now or at His second coming, every person who trusts Him will be healed completely.

What we CANNOT do is to say that because some people are not healed, that it invalidates any healing at all in Jesus' name and by the power of the Holy Spirit.[6] We cannot accept that one person's lack of healing should keep us from pursuing God's grace for healing others.

In the atonement, Jesus paid the price for all sin, and yet for whatever reason, some people still do not get saved. The fact that some people still die and go to hell does not nullify that Jesus is the Savior of the world or that the church has the job of evangelizing. In the same way, the fact that some people are not healed does not invalidate the commission on the church to continue praying to heal the sick.

A Scholarly Explanation

I don't want to dwell long on this point, but I do appreciate how Sam Storms, in his article "Divine Healing," speaks on this issue:

> "Everything we receive from God finds its ultimate source in what Christ did for us on the cross. Therefore, the question is not whether our bodies receive healing because of the atonement of Christ, but when. We are forgiven of our sins now because of Christ's atoning death, but we await the consummation of our deliverance from the presence of sin when Christ returns. We experience fellowship with God now because of Christ's atoning death, but we await the consummation of that blessed relationship when Christ returns. We profit immensely now from the Spirit's work in our hearts, but who would dare suggest that what the Holy Spirit is doing in this age is all that he will ever do? There is a glorious harvest reserved in heaven for us of which the present ministry of the Holy Spirit is merely the first fruits!
>
> In other words, it is a serious mistake for us to think that every blessing Christ secured through his redemptive suffering will be ours now in its consummate form. All

such blessings shall indeed be ours, let there be no mistake about that. But let us not expect, far less demand, that we now experience fully those blessings which God has clearly reserved for heaven in the age to come..."[7]

He goes on to say:

"To insist that this physical blessing is future is not to detract from the efficacy or value of Christ's atoning work, nor to deny that God often heals (at times partially, at times wholly) now. It is simply to recognize, as Scripture does, that God's timing is often different from ours."

So What Do We Do?

I 100% believe that Jesus is still our Healer. I believe this from the Bible. I believe this from church history. And I believe it from many personal experiences with healing today.

Does everyone get healed? No. However, I am not discouraged by that to the point that I would stop praying for the sick and going after the Lord for more![8]

We must learn to pursue Jesus Christ to heal ALL of our diseases now, with full faith in His atoning work and an unending hope for His miraculous intervention immediately.

We do not need to pray, "Lord, if it is Your will, heal..." He has made it evident that it is His will to heal. We must learn to pray, instead, "Lord, let your Kingdom come; let your *healing* be done, on earth (now) as it is (now) in heaven."[9]

As many respected, charismatic leaders have said concerning the "already but not yet": it is not a matter of "IF" we can see God's Kingdom power now; it is a matter of "HOW MUCH?" can we have on this side of eternity. To find out the answer, we must believe what He says and pursue Him for healing, in faith, for every sickness and disease we encounter.

So what do we do? We lay hands on the sick, pray the prayer of faith, and believe God will be faithful to His promise. The rest is up to Him.

Endnotes

[1] Philippians 2:5-8

[2] Matthew 10:1, 5-8

[3] Luke 10:1-2a,8-9

[4] Matthew 28:18-20 (emphasis mine)

[5] Mark 16:15-18

[6] This would base our theology on experience rather than on scriptures — the charge often brought by cessationists against charismatic believers.

[7] Storms, Sam. *Divine Healing.* Oklahoma City, OK: Sam Storms, 2006.

[8] Luke 11:13

[9] Paraphrase of Matthew 6:10.

| 3 |

Atonement, Authority, and Anointing

In the last chapter, we discussed the issue of whether or not Christian healing is for today. Concluding that there is no biblical expectation that this (or any) spiritual gift would cease in the first century, we must now turn our attention to the practice of Christian healing. In the next few chapters, we will begin to lay a foundation for how we can actively be involved in the healing ministry ourselves.

We will look practically at both the believer's authority to heal and the Holy Spirit's anointing to heal. First, however, we need to look at these two things side by side and understand how they flow out of the atonement of Jesus to get a full picture of how they are separate but mutually dependent on one another.

Healing was Anticipated in the Promise of Messiah

It could be argued that the promise of healing began in the Old Testament as soon as sin entered the world. Remember, through the *protoevangelion* (first gospel) in Genesis 3:16, God promises a redeemer who would crush the head of the serpent and undo all the effects of sin. As sickness was introduced through the fall of man, healing is a necessary part of the restoration God would bring through His coming Savior.

Throughout the Old Testament, this promise of healing is repeatedly tied to the Messiah who would save the world from sin, heal their sicknesses and disease, and deliver humanity from bondage to the devil and his kingdom of darkness.

In the previous chapters, we have already looked at God's revealed name of Jehovah Rapha and the promise of healing in passages like Psalm 103 and Isaiah 53. We won't take time to do that again here. Instead, we will look briefly at the three A's of healing: Atonement, Authority, and Anointing.

Healing Starts in The Atonement

The realization of all of God's promises came through the sinless life, sacrificial death, and resurrection of Jesus. This is stated explicitly in 2 Corinthians 1:19-20:

> *"For the Son of God, Jesus Christ, whom we proclaimed among you... was not Yes and No, but in him it is always Yes. For all the*

promises of God find their Yes in him. That is why it is through him that we utter our Amen to God for his glory."

Therefore, it comes as no surprise that Jesus stood in the synagogue at Nazareth and declared that He was the fulfillment of all Messianic prophecy, specifically those listed in Isaiah 61.[1] We have looked at those verses already in Chapter 1.

We must understand that the things Isaiah prophesied that the coming Messiah would do are simply a summary of God's plan to fully reverse the Fall of Man.

When we speak of Christ's atonement, then, we are discussing the extent to which Jesus would carry the weight of human sin and suffering on Himself to restore us to God's original plan and perfection.

"Sozo" - Complete Salvation

Even the Greek word for "saved" in the New Testament — "*sozo*" — is an all-encompassing term for the fulfillment of the promises found in Jesus' atonement! (What a great name for a ministry[2]...)

The Concise Greek-English Dictionary of the New Testament[3] defines sozo this way:

> σῴζω – save (of Christian salvation); save, rescue, deliver; keep safe, preserve; cure, make well.

To make it as simple as possible: the atonement of Jesus Christ offers 'complete salvation' to those who come to Him by faith. That is salvation from sin, healing in their physical bodies, and deliverance from the power of their enemy, the Devil. To remove any one of these fulfilled promises from Christian salvation is to remove power from the cross!

Healing Authority is Your Inheritance

Knowing that Jesus purchased our healing in His atonement on the cross, we then turned our attention to the fact that He passed the authority to heal on to His first apostles (Matthew 10:1), other disciples (Luke 10:1-9), and then to the whole church (Matthew 28:18-20).

He did not just talk about healing as something only He could give. Rather, He commanded believers to put that authority into action by healing the sick. Just as He spoke to diseases to leave and ordered bodies to be restored, He commanded His followers to do the same. This command was clearly one which the New Testament expected to continue throughout the church age (Mark 16:15-18).

All believers have been promised healing in our own bodies AND been given the authority to extend Christ's healing to others who come by faith and receive. It is a universal promise within the body of Christ!

Healing Anointing Multiplies the Fruit

The authority of all believers to heal in Jesus' name is amazing enough, but that is not the full extent of Christian healing in the New Testament! As my spiritual overseer, Dr. Randy Clark, always says, "there is more!"

As I have sought the Lord to understand the healing gift, the Holy Spirit spoke to me recently saying: *"While all believers have the authority to command healing, and all believers carry the inheritance of My atonement – salvation, healing, and deliverance – the 'charis' gift of healing, and the anointing to heal is reserved for those who are hungry and pursuing."*

He explained to me that although the authority to heal is there for all people, it is through the anointing of the Holy Spirit that He amplifies everything His blood purchased, "on earth as it is in heaven." Yet, it is up to us to seek Him for more of His anointing.

Remember, before Jesus left the earth, He had already given the disciples authority, yet he told them to wait for the Holy Spirit to empower them before they began to minister:

> *"And while staying with them he ordered them not to depart from Jerusalem, but to wait for the promise of the Father, which, he said, 'you heard from me; for John baptized with water, but you will be baptized with the Holy Spirit not many days from now... but you will receive power when the Holy Spirit has come upon you, and you will be my witnesses in Jerusalem and in all Judea and Samaria, and to the end of the earth.'"*[4]

It is through the empowering of the Holy Spirit which God releases His special grace-gifts into His church. As we seek Him for His anointing to heal, there is a compounding effect on how much fruit we are able to bear.

Simply put, while all believers can heal sick people, we should expect even more people will be healed as we pursue — and receive — the power of God in the Holy Spirit and receive the "gifts of healing" He distributes to His church!

This is what I discovered early on in my journey into the healing ministry. There is a common grace for healing in the church (authority), yet the easiest way to see fruit is to partner our authority with His anointing.

After the prayer of impartation from Dr. Clark, I received a Holy Spirit anointing to heal the sick. Immediately I saw blind eyes opened, the lame walk, and since then, the healing miracles have continued to increase in my ministry and more.

Endnotes

[1] Luke 4:16-21

[2] For those who may not know, I oversee a ministry called Sozo Ministries International. You can find out more at www.SozoMinistries.net.

[3] Newman, B.M., Jr., 1993. A Concise Greek-English dictionary of the New Testament.

[4] Acts 1:4-5,8

| 4 |

The Believer's Authority

In the last chapter, we looked at a general overview of healing in the atonement, in the believer's authority in Christ, and through the anointing of the Holy Spirit. We will now look a little closer at the authority all Christians have for healing, then come back to the Spirit's atonement a little bit later.

In laying the foundation for the believer's authority to heal, there are two areas we must discuss. The first is our own beliefs and expectations concerning our authority to heal, which we will discuss in this chapter. Then, we will look at how we put that authority into practice in the next.

The Basis of Our Authority to Heal

Jesus made a very casual statement in the book of John, which has been the topic of much disagreement between Christians for millennia. However, as you know, my general approach is to take the Bible at its word unless there is something to imply there is more behind what is stated. In this case, there does not seem to be a hidden meaning.

Jesus' statement was this:

> *"Truly, truly, I say to you, whoever believes in me will also do the works that I do; and greater works than these will he do, because I am going to the Father."*[1]

This verse follows after an explanation that everything Jesus was doing was not on His own authority but an extension of the authority of God[2]. He then gives us His radical expectation that if a person would simply believe in Him, that person will also do what He does!

As we have previously discussed, the things that Jesus did were to fulfill all the Messianic prophecies he quotes in Luke 4:18-19. One of these Messianic promises, which he was fulfilling daily when He made this statement, was healing the sick. Now He says here that He expects His disciples' belief in Him to translate into their doing the same thing! Put simply, if He healed the sick, then through our faith in Him, we should be healing the sick!

The Name of Jesus – Our Place of Authority

Looking again at John 14, Jesus goes on to say:

> *"Whatever you ask in my name, this I will do, that the Father may be glorified in the Son. If you ask me anything in my name, I will do it."*[3]

From this passage of scripture alone, it is easy for the human mind to race with unlimited possibilities. After all, Jesus said, "whatever you ask," I will do. Unfortunately, though, within the passage itself, there is a limitation on the scope of this promise. It does not mean we can ask Jesus for a new Land Rover or a million dollars and simply wait for it to come.

His statement that He would do "whatever we ask" was directly tied to us accomplishing the same works that He was doing by the Father's authority! He is implying a chain of command!

Jesus' Authority Becomes Our Authority

God commanded Jesus to heal the sick in fulfillment of His promises (see John 5:19). That command carries with it the authority of the One giving it. In the same way, Jesus commands those who would believe in Him to continue doing His work – including healing the sick. This command, therefore, must carry the same authority from God to do so. This is why when we pray for the sick, we pray "in Jesus' name."

That phrase — "in Jesus' name" — means that we are praying as someone who has a right to be heard in the heavenlies because we have Jesus' authority backing us up! It is the same as when a police officer shouts, "stop in the name of the law," or when a judge places his name on a court order. The name of the one in authority is what validates the command, even when someone else is the one enacting it!

What we must come to understand and believe is that Jesus gave His own authority to the church to continue the works He began, and He expects them to continue "in His name!"

Jesus Gave His Authority (Before He Gave His Holy Spirit)

Most people look at healing and think, "Well, I don't have that gift" or "God can do whatever He wants to do. It's not up to me." This is NOT a correct attitude, however. This is why I said we must first fix our belief system before talking about the practice of healing itself!

Do you realize that Jesus' first commissioning on His disciples was not an impartation of the Holy Spirit — He would not impart the Holy Spirit to them until after the resurrection in John 20:22, and then again at Pentecost. His first commissioning was an impartation of His authority. As Matthew writes,

> *"And he called to him his twelve disciples and gave them authority over unclean spirits, to cast them out, and to heal every disease and every affliction."*[4]

After listing the names of the 12, it goes on:

> *"These twelve Jesus sent out, instructing them, "Go nowhere among the Gentiles and enter no town of the Samaritans, but go*

rather to the lost sheep of the house of Israel. And proclaim as you go, saying, 'The kingdom of heaven is at hand.' Heal the sick, raise the dead, cleanse lepers, cast out demons. You received without paying; give without pay."[5]

Jesus did not tell the disciples to go and "pray for the sick." Instead, he told them to heal them! The disciples did this through the authority they had been given!

In Luke 10, Jesus "appoints" 72 others with the same authority and the same commissioning!

"Whenever you enter a town and they receive you, eat what is set before you. Heal the sick in it and say to them, 'The kingdom of God has come near to you."[6]

I believe these instructions — proclaim the gospel, heal the sick, and cast out demons — are primarily what Jesus is referencing in Matthew 28 when He says, "teaching them to obey everything I have commanded you," in the Great Commission. This is also validated by Marks' rendering of the Great Commission in Mark 16.

"...And these signs will accompany those who believe: in my name they will cast out demons; they will speak in new tongues; they will pick up serpents with their hands; and if they drink any deadly poison, it will not hurt them; they will lay their hands on the sick, and they will recover."[7]

It is Your Authority to Heal

You may be asking, "why does any of this matter?" After all, haven't we already laid a foundation and know that healing still happens today from the last few chapters?

Yes! But the point I want to make is that not only does healing still happen but that YOU, as a believer, have been given the authority to heal the sick. It is not someone else's job.

The bible says that "all may prophesy," not just the prophets (see 1 Corinthians 14:31). It also instructs that all believers are to "do the work of an evangelist," not just those with the gift of evangelism (see 2 Timothy 4:5). In the same way, the Bible teaches that all believers have authority over sickness and disease in Jesus Christ! However, we MUST believe in this truth before we can effectively operate in healing.

The Necessity of Faith

The Bible makes it very clear that there is a direct link between our belief and our authority to heal. Before we can begin "doing" what Jesus did, we must first do the harder work of "believing" what Jesus said.

Over and over again, the Bible tells us that it is belief that matters. One example is in the book of James:

> *"Is anyone among you sick?... the prayer of faith will save the one who is sick, and the Lord will raise him up..."*[8]

In another story, Jesus comes out of His private prayer time and finds the disciples unable to heal a child with a demonically-caused epilepsy. After He heals the child, the disciples ask why they weren't able to do so. Jesus answers:

> *"He said to them, 'Because of your little faith. For truly, I say to you, if you have faith like a grain of mustard seed, you will say to this mountain, 'Move from here to there,' and it will move, and nothing will be impossible for you.'"*[9]

When Mark shares his version of this same story, the family demands to know if Jesus can heal their child after his disciples had failed. Jesus reassures them:

(The boy's father said) "But if you can do anything, have compassion on us and help us." And Jesus said to him, "'If you can'! All things are possible for one who believes."[10]

The Faith of the Sick Person

From this last verse, it seems that not only does Jesus place the onus of faith on the one doing the healing, but He also includes the faith of the sick to be healed, as well as those in the crowd around Him!

It is true that not only the faith of the one praying matters. After all, how many times do we see Jesus, the one who IS God, not base His authority for healing on Himself, but also on those He is ministering to? How often do we hear Him say the words, "Your Faith has made you well"? (See Luke 8:48, 17:19, 18:42, Mark 5:34, 10:52, and Matthew 9:22 for examples).

Still, I would caution putting too much emphasis on the faith of others, though, as you practice your own authority to heal. After all, when Jesus went to Nazareth — the faithless city — the Bible says:

> *"And he could do no mighty work there, except that he laid his hands on a few sick people and healed them. And he marveled because of their unbelief. And he went about among the villages teaching."*[11]

Even when he could do no great miracles due to the people's lack of faith, Jesus' authority to heal the sick was still working!

I will add that in my own experience, some of the most radical healings I have seen have been while praying for people who didn't believe and/or being surrounded by unbelievers.

You Have The Authority of Christ to Heal

Your authority to heal is dependent on your ability to believe. This belief is prerequisite to the power of the Holy Spirit working inside you[12]. Again, I believe both are necessary; yet you cannot deny that in the examples we have shared in this chapter, Jesus and those He personally trained[13] healed people by their authority more than by their anointing!

Yes, there are those who are given a special anointing to heal, but healing in the Bible is not just a gift of the Spirit. It is a part of your inheritance in Christ. It is within your authority as a representative of heaven on earth. All you must do is believe it in order to see it.

Endnotes

[1] John 14:12

[2] John 14:10

[3] John 14:13-14

[4] Matthew 10:1

[5] Matthew 10:5-8

[6] Luke 10:8-9

[7] Mark 16:17-18

[8] James 5:14-15

[9] Matthew 17:20

[10] Mark 9:23

[11] Mark 6:5-6

[12] It is likely that many of us are anointed by the Holy Spirit to do much more than we are currently experiencing, but we are missing out because we do not have the faith for it.

[13] The 12 apostles were healing the sick by authority long before Jesus blew on them to receive the Holy Spirit!

| 5 |

Healing By Command

In the last chapter, we discussed the believer's authority to heal and how that authority transferred from God, through Jesus, to His disciples and the church. We said that the fruit of the believer's authority is linked directly to the believer's level of belief in God's desire to heal. In this chapter, we will now turn our attention to the practical side of our authority to heal and discuss how it is our privilege to command sickness and disease to leave, in Jesus' name.

Jesus Healed By Authority

Once again, we must look first to Jesus as our example in healing the sick and practicing authority. What stands out to me is that in the gospels, whenever Jesus healed the sick, it was always accomplished in one of two ways. He either healed by physical touch, or he healed by commanding the disease to leave.

The act of laying on of hands in scripture is always a physical outworking of the anointing of God on a person through the power of the Holy Spirit. Therefore, when Jesus laid hands on someone, I believe it was a practical example of healing through the anointing, which we will discuss in the next few chapters.

For now, I want to focus on Jesus' practice of commanding or rebuking sickness in people's bodies, which, instead of demonstrating His anointing, was a manifestation of His authority over the power of sickness and death.

Commanding Sickness is Demonstrated by Jesus

Over and over again in the Bible, when Jesus heals the sick, we see Him do it through a verbal command, either toward the sickness itself, towards a person's body, or towards a demonic spirit that was causing the disease.

Jesus Commanded Diseases to Go

One of my favorite phrases in the New Testament is "...Jesus rebuked..." This is used in reference to all sorts of earthly phenomenons, such as calming storms, yet most commonly, we hear it regarding sickness. For example, not long into His earthly ministry, Jesus meets Simon Peter's mother-in-law, who has been sick for some time.

> *"And he arose and left the synagogue and entered Simon's house. Now Simon's mother-in-law was ill with a high fever, and they appealed to him on her behalf. And he stood over her and* ***re-***

> ***buked the fever, and it left her,*** *and immediately she rose and began to serve them."*[1]

Jesus doesn't pray for the woman. He doesn't implore God to heal her. Instead, He speaks directly to the disease and commands it to leave her body. In His authority from God, He spoke, and the disease responded by leaving!

Remember, Jesus said that He did nothing, except what God revealed to Him to do (John 5:19). That means that as Jesus healed every sick person around Him, it was God's will being fulfilled!

Jesus Commanded Bodies to Receive Healing

Not only do we see Jesus rebuking disease. We also see Him speaking to people's bodies, commanding them to recover from their physically broken state. Take, for example, His healing of the blind man, Bartimeus:

> *"And Jesus stopped and commanded him to be brought to him. And when he came near, he asked him, "What do you want me to do for you?" He said, "Lord, let me recover my sight." And* ***Jesus said to him, "Recover your sight****; your faith has made you well." And immediately he recovered his sight and followed him, glorifying God. And all the people, when they saw it, gave praise to God."*[2]

As Jesus spoke to bodies, they responded to His authority and recovered.

Jesus Commanded Demons to Leave

Another demonstration of Jesus' authority to heal people was in His rebuke of demonic spirits, which were causing sicknesses and diseases. Remember, disease and demonic torments are both results of humanity's fall into sin. Therefore, the sinless Son of Man has authority over all these things. Take the example we discussed in the last chapter, of Jesus healing the epileptic boy after His disciples could not:

> *"While (Jesus) was coming, the demon threw (the boy) to the ground and convulsed him. But* ***Jesus rebuked the unclean spirit and healed the boy****, and gave him back to his father."*[3]

In Jesus' ministry, we see Him commanding disease to leave in all forms! Jesus commanded invasive sicknesses, like viruses and infections, to get out of people's bodies. He spoke to people's bodies to be healed of their own brokenness, like blindness and deafness. He also took authority in the spirit realm, where many people's afflictions were caused, and not only healed them but also got rid of the tormenting spirits.

Jesus' Disciples Also Healed by Command

From this discussion, we might well conclude that Jesus' authority to heal was all-encompassing! That is true, and the good news is that it did not stop with Jesus. When He gave His authority to His disciples, they responded by practicing their authority in the same ways He did.

Jesus' Disciples Commanded Diseases to Go

As we have already looked at previously, the Bible records that before Jesus ever gave His Holy Spirit to the disciples, He transferred His God-given authority over sickness and disease to them!

> *"And he called the twelve together and gave them power and authority over all demons and to cure diseases, and he sent them out to proclaim the kingdom of God and to heal... And they departed and went through the villages, preaching the gospel and healing everywhere."*[4]

Although this verse doesn't specifically say they "rebuked the sicknesses" verbally, there is no implication in Jesus' command or in their practice that says they were praying for the sick and asking God to heal. It was the disciples who were healing with the authority Jesus gave them. As Jewish disciples following a Rabbi, they most likely did this the same way He had demonstrated.

Even after Jesus left this earth and gave them the Holy Spirit at Pentecost, the Bible still records that the Apostles were the ones active in healing people. They were not praying and asking God to do it.

> *"Now many signs and wonders were regularly done among the people by the hands of the apostles (i.e. not by the hand of God). And they were all together in Solomon's Portico...The people also gath-*

ered from the towns around Jerusalem, bringing the sick and those afflicted with unclean spirits, and they were all healed."[5]

Jesus' Disciples Commanded Bodies to Receive Healing

In the same way that Jesus spoke to people's bodies to recover, the Bible records the disciples doing so as well. One example is the first miracle after Jesus gave the Great Commission and left. While going to the temple to pray, Peter and John healed the lame beggar, sitting at the gate of the temple courts:

> *"But Peter said, 'I have no silver and gold, but what I do have I give to you. In the name of Jesus Christ of Nazareth, rise up and walk!"*[6]

Peter spoke with authority, in Jesus' name, and commanded the man's body to function correctly. And it did!

Jesus' Disciples Commanded Demons to Leave

Not to leave anything out — remember, Jesus promised that all who believe in Him would do the same works that He did (John 14:12) — the bible also records that the disciples, too, cast out demonic spirits that were tormenting and afflicting people. Take the story of Paul, who was being followed around by a demon-possessed girl:

> *"And this she kept doing for many days. Paul, having become greatly annoyed, turned and said to the spirit, 'I command you in the name of Jesus Christ to come out of her.' And it came out that very hour."*[7]

The disciples of Jesus demonstrated the same authority as Jesus by commanding sickness, bodily afflictions, and demons, "in Jesus name!"

The Authority to Command "In Jesus' Name"

This brings us back to the point we made before: Jesus said in John 14:

> *"Whatever you ask in my name, this I will do, that the Father may be glorified in the Son."*[8]

The authority of a believer today does not come from within ourselves, and it cannot be something we claim for ourselves. Our authority is explicitly given to us by Jesus, the same as it was to His disciples, and therefore we can only accomplish the things He commanded us to do by doing them "*in His name.*" It is the name of Jesus that is our 'badge' of authority.

When Peter was called to the authorities and had to explain the healing of the lame man mentioned above, he goes out of his way to explain that it was not his own authority, but that of Christ, that the man was healed:

"And (Jesus') name — by faith in his name — made this man strong whom you see and know, and the faith that is through Jesus has given the man this perfect health in the presence of you all."[9]

One of my favorite scriptures in the Bible is when the governing authorities take note and wonder how this authority must have come from Jesus because these men on their own were nothing:

"Now when they saw the boldness of Peter and John, and perceived that they were uneducated, common men, they were astonished. And ***they recognized that they had been with Jesus.****"*[10]

Later, as the church prayed for more boldness to continue doing what Jesus had commanded them, it is clear that they understood there was a distinction between the hand of God working sovereignly and what was being done through them by the authority in His name:

"And now, Lord, look upon their threats and grant to your servants to continue to speak your word with all boldness, while you stretch out your hand to heal, and signs and wonders are performed through the name of your holy servant Jesus."[11]

The Authority for Healing Continues in the Church

Knowing that Jesus passed His authority to His apostles and the other early disciples and that He expected His Kingdom and authority to continue to grow in the earth (Isaiah 9:7), it should not be surprising that Jesus' stated intention was that His authority would remain with His people, the church, until His second coming!

Authority is in the Great Commission

Once again, this command to "heal the sick" — complete with His authority to do so — continued in the church after His departure. It is an inseparable part of the Great Commission.

> *"And these signs will accompany those who believe: in my name they will cast out demons; they will speak in new tongues; they will pick up serpents with their hands; and if they drink any deadly poison, it will not hurt them; they will lay their hands on the sick, and they will recover."*[12]

Although I cannot possibly give a full account in this small book, I can boldly say that Christian history has recorded healing in EVERY branch of the church in EVERY generation since Jesus spoke the Great Commission. Even in the most cessationist denominations, time is occasionally given to pray for the sick, and (occasionally) healing miracles have been recorded by all of them.

God is Glorified by Our Practicing Authority "in Jesus' Name"

The Bible is clear of Jesus' intention that believers would use the authority given by Christ to the church. This is not an abuse or a misuse of His power. It is how He gets glory! We need to practice doing what He said even more.

> *"And whatever you do, in word or deed, do everything in the name of the Lord Jesus, giving thanks to God the Father through him."*[13]

The Great Controversy: Can Man Tell God What to Do?

One of the biggest criticisms against those who practice their authority in Christian healing is that *"these healers command God, telling Him what to do."*

If that were the case, I would agree with the critics that it would demonstrate the utmost arrogance by mere men, elevating themselves above God Himself. However, from my own experience in the healing ministry and in my observation of dozens of other healing ministers, both contemporary and historical, this is a major misunderstanding by the critics of the practice of healing.

I have never seen a credible healing minister command God to do anything! Yes, they do make commands, but God is not the target; sickness is. This is the same as it was for Jesus and the early disciples. Even though this practice is often called a "prayer of command," the truth is that this is not really a prayer to God, petitioning Him to move. Instead, this is an exhibition of the believer's authority, which Jesus Himself first demonstrated.

When speaking in training conferences and discipling believers to pray for the sick, I am always diligent to make this distinction clear. We ask God to heal, and we command sickness to go. We can't get this confused. We do not ask sickness to go — *'oh cancer, please, if it be your will, leave this body...'* — nor do we ever command God to do anything — *'Lord, I command You to remove this cancer...'* To do those things would lead to devastating results in the pursuit of healing and would bring a major level of sin into our relationship with the Lord.

However, as we are careful to point our commands appropriately, it is a practice as old as the New Testament for believers to speak to sickness in the name of Jesus and command it to go.

It's Time to Use Your Authority

If you are a believer in Jesus Christ, you have been given His authority as His representative in the earth. In His name, you have the right to speak to every manner of sickness, affliction, and demonic torment and command them to go! What is lacking is a motivation among God's people to do what Jesus told us to do, either due to a lack of understanding and belief or a lack of boldness to operate in our authority.

If you lack belief, then please go back and read the previous chapters, dig into scripture, and see what Jesus says you carry. If you lack boldness, then do as the early church did, and pray for God to give you more. However, to be faithful to Jesus' command to heal the sick, you are eventually going to have to look at the sickness in front of you and command it to go, "in Jesus' name."

As John Wimber is often credited with saying, "faith is spelled R-I-S-K." It is one of those things that you will never know until you try! I cannot guarantee anything concerning your efforts. There are often other, unseen realities at work that may prevent healing from coming immediately, yet that is not an excuse to not make an attempt!

Jesus wants the sick to be healed, and He wants you to be the one doing it. So go for it! "In Jesus' name," tell those diseases to get out and not come back. (Then please share your testimony with me[14], so we can celebrate and give glory to God together)

Endnotes

[1] Luke 4:38-39 (emphasis mine)
[2] Luke 18:40-43 (emphasis mine)
[3] Luke 9:42 (emphasis mine)
[4] Luke 9:1 and 6
[5] Acts 5:12 and 16 (emphasis mine)
[6] Acts 3:6
[7] Acts 16:18
[8] John 14:13
[9] Acts 3:16
[10] John 4:13
[11] Acts 4:29-30
[12] Mark 16:17-18

[13] Colossians 3:17

[14]Email me at blog@anthonyingram.com

| 6 |

The Spirit's Anointing

We will now begin to shift the focus from all believers' *authority* to heal and begin to look at the special *anointing* for healing given to some. In this chapter and the next, we will discuss how the Holy Spirit's empowerment escalates a believer's authority and effectiveness for the church age through the "gifts of healing" spoken of by the Apostle Paul in His letter to the Corinthian church.

Understanding God's Anointing

Right before Jesus left this earth, He told his disciples:

"But you will receive power when the Holy Spirit has come upon you, and you will be my witnesses in Jerusalem and in all Judea and Samaria, and to the end of the earth."[1]

This "power" was something different than the "authority" which He had already given them to proclaim His Kingdom, heal the sick, and cast out demons (Matthew 10:1). This power was something new; something they had not yet experienced.

In the Greek text, the word "authority" is "*exousia*" which, according to one dictionary, means *"a state of control over something"* or the ability to *"command, control or govern."*[2]

This is in direct contrast to the word for "power," which is "*dynamai*" in Acts 1:8, which comes from the root word "*dunamis.*" According to the same dictionary, this word means the *"potential for functioning in some way, power, might, strength, force, capability... specifically, the power that works wonders."* This Greek word is where we get our English word, dynamite. This is explosive power, much bigger than can be contained in ourselves.

I have stated before that while both of these are gifts for believers which come from God, they are received in different ways. Jesus gives authority to all believers as part of our inheritance in Him. This is why He can command His disciples to command others to do the same things He commissioned them to do (Matthew 28:18-20).

Power, on the other hand, is given through the anointing of the Holy Spirit, and each believer receives different aspects of His anointing, as their specific needs, callings, and even pursuits will determine. While all have the authority to heal, not everyone will have His anointing for the healing gift.

How the Anointing Comes

Jesus directly tied the power-anointing to the coming of the Holy Spirit. This was something He had promised many times in His earthly ministry. (See, for instance, John 16:4-15.) Whereas Jesus was Emmanuel – "God *with* us" – the Holy Spirit's presence would be different. He would be "God *in* us." This would be the divine union of God and mankind, which up to that point had only been seen in a select few prophets and leaders in Israel's history. This would be the fulfillment of Joel's prophecy:

> *"And it shall come to pass afterward, that I will pour out my Spirit on all flesh; your sons and your daughters shall prophesy, your old men shall dream dreams, and your young men shall see visions. Even on the male and female servants in those days I will pour out my Spirit."*[3]

As Jesus left the earth, His final instruction to the disciples was to wait in Jerusalem for the Holy Spirit to bring this anointing on them (Acts 1:4).

The Day of Pentecost

Finally, on the day of Pentecost, 40 days after Jesus had been crucified for the sin of the world, God released the Holy Spirit on His church with that power. We read about this in Acts 2:

> *When the day of Pentecost arrived, they were all together in one place. And suddenly there came from heaven a sound like a mighty rushing wind, and it filled the entire house where they were sitting. And divided tongues as of fire appeared to them and rested on each one of them. And they were all filled with the Holy Spirit and began to speak in other tongues as the Spirit gave them utterance.*[4]

As they take this Holy Spirit party to the streets, there is a lot of commotion in the crowd. People are hearing these uneducated Jews speaking in various languages, proclaiming the Kingdom of God. This spectacle was too much for many in the crowds, leading some to believe they were drunk and rambling, but Peter stands up and announces that this is the fulfillment of Joel's prophecy.

In a matter of minutes, this new power from on High escalated the effectiveness of the Apostles' ministries beyond anything they had seen before, and that day, over 3000 people chose to give their lives to Christ.

The Power Gifts

As time went on, the Apostles learned to follow the Holy Spirit's leading and came to understand more about ministry under His anointing. They began to share this knowledge among the churches. The most famous passage regarding the Holy Spirit and His giftings was from the Apostle Paul to the church at Corinth:

> *Now concerning spiritual gifts, brothers, I do not want you to be uninformed... Now there are varieties of gifts, but the same Spirit; and there are varieties of service, but the same Lord; and there are varieties of activities, but it is the same God who empowers them all in everyone. To each is given the manifestation of the Spirit for the common good.*[5]

Paul lists 9 particular gifts He had seen in use (though other gifts are listed elsewhere in the Bible.) These gifts are:

- words of wisdom
- words of knowledge
- gifts of faith
- gifts of healing
- working of miracles
- prophetic utterances
- discerning of spirits
- various forms of tongues
- interpretation of unknown tongues.

The word for "gifts" here is the Greek word "*charis*" or "*charismata*" which can be interpreted as "grace" or "grace-gifts." The dictionary refers to them as *"special gifts of a non-material sort, bestowed through God's generosity on individual Christians."*[6] It is from this word for gifts that we get our word "charismatic."

Everyone Gets Power; Just Not The Same Gifts

Paul makes it clear that although all believers were to be filled with the Holy Spirit and walk in His power, the particular gifting each one receives would be determined on an individual basis.

While it is impossible to clearly articulate all the reasons God would choose to give some gifts to certain believers and not to others, I do believe scripture gives us some clear understanding of a few of these reasons.

Gifted For Our Calling

The first reason is that our gifts will likely be suited to our specific calling in God's service. For instance, scripture seems to record that the first Apostles were able, at times, to act in every one of the gifts, though they likely did not walk in every gift all the time. In each situation, different aspects of the anointing would come into use as needed. This makes sense since the Apostles were foundational in establishing every part of the church.

It, therefore, makes sense to me that other callings would also receive gifts from the Holy Spirit, specific to their role in the body. For example, I think of evangelists who work primarily with non-believers. Their calling would likely make use of gifts of prophecy, healing, or working miracles, to demonstrate the power of God. On the other hand, pastors might be better served by gifts like words of knowledge or words of wisdom, as they instruct the body of Christ to become more like Jesus. Intercessory callings, as well, would need gifts like tongues and interpretation of tongues.

I know that I am speaking hypothetically, as I cannot prove this theory from scripture. However, I have studied and sat in seminars on spiritual gifts, and I have heard many ministers discussing how certain gifts function well together to fulfill God's assignments. For example, Dr. Randy Clark specifically ties the gift of healing to receiving words of knowledge.[7]

Gifted for Our Season

The second reason a person might get particular gifts is based on the season God created that person to minister in.

History has taught us that although all of the gifts of the Spirit have been active in every age, there are seasons in which some gifts take priority on the larger, global stage. Think about the great healing revival that took place in the U.S. and spread around the world in the 1950s or the restoration movement of the prophetic gifting in the 1980s. Other gifts were still taking place in those seasons, but as God gifted certain ministers with stronger anointings in these giftings, it was directly linked to what He was doing on a large scale in that season. His global purposes in those seasons demanded more of one particular gifting than others.

Gifted Through Impartation

A third way a person receives particular giftings is through the transference of anointing from another minister. The laying on of hands is a foundational teaching of the church (see Hebrews 6:1-2), and is a major way, biblically, by which we see spiritual gifts being released into people's lives. For example, Paul tells Timothy:

"Do not neglect the gift you have, which was given you by prophecy when the council of elders laid their hands on you."[8]

Later he writes,

"For this reason I remind you to fan into flame the gift of God, which is in you through the laying on of my hands"[9]

Paul also writes to the Romans that he desires to come to see them in person to "impart" some spiritual gift to them.[10] I think it is safe to assume this impartation would occur in the same manner - by laying on of hands.

Gifted Because of Our Desires

A fourth determining factor, and the one I put a lot more stock in than some of the others, is that God distributes His giftings based on the passions and desires of the one receiving.

Paul says in 1 Corinthians 14:1,

"Pursue love, and earnestly desire the spiritual gifts, especially that you may prophesy."

And again in verse 39,

"So, my brothers, earnestly desire to prophesy..."

If Paul, two chapters earlier, tells us that gifts are given at the sole discretion of the Holy Spirit, why then would he tell the believers to "*desire*" specific gifts unless their desire plays into the gifts they receive?

The word "desire" means to "*be positively and intensely interested in something, strive, desire, exert oneself earnestly, be dedicated*"[11] to that thing. It carries the weight of English words like "be jealous for," "burn with desire for," or even "to lust after" (if it is possible to read the word lust without a sinful connotation).

Paul tells us very clearly that the Holy Spirit determines which gifts we get, and therefore, we need to live with such passion for His works in our lives that He will freely give us the gifts we are seeking in service to Him.

Jesus Himself said,

> *"For everyone who asks receives, and the one who seeks finds, and to the one who knocks it will be opened. Or which one of you, if his son asks him for bread, will give him a stone? Or if he asks for a fish, will give him a serpent? If you then, who are evil, know how to give good gifts to your children, how much more will your Father who is in heaven give good things to those who ask him!"*[12]

As a good Father, God responds to our desires when they are glorifying to Him.

Seeking an Anointing for Healing

To bring our focus back to the matter at hand — an anointing for healing — I think there is one undeniable way a person can receive an anointing for healing from the Lord: Go out and pray for the sick!

You can pray for the gift. You can study the gift. You can read books and blog posts on healing. You can follow others with the gift of healing. You can attend healing schools and healing conferences. And all of those things may be helpful to you in one way or another, but until you begin to actually step out in such a way that it allows the Holy Spirit an opportunity to anoint you and use you for healing, it will never happen.

The healing anointing comes when we are actually seeking God's power to heal by praying for the sick. That is how we show the Lord we are serious. We take the risk and expect Him to meet us in the moment.

In my experience, when we desire to serve His Kingdom with His power and gifts, He makes a way for us to grow in those gifts and anointing. As I share in the appendix to this book, I was praying for the sick every week, for months, when I lived in Haiti, and no one was getting healed. I began reading books and watching videos, trying to learn more about how He works this gift, and God met me through it all. My desire for healing moved God's heart, and He directed me to Dr. Randy Clark's conference — Voice of the Apostles — where I received an impartation. I began seeing healing the next week when a blind man in South Sudan received his healing. The gifting has continued to increase exponentially since that time through my continued efforts to pray for those in need of healing.

What About You?

In the next chapter, we will look specifically at the "gift of healing" and how it works in the body of Christ. For now, I want to ask you: what gift of the Holy Spirit are you burning for? If you could have any of His power gifts discussed in scripture, which one would it be, and why? Are you pursuing it? Are you studying how the gift works and looking for opportunities to learn from others in that area? Are you taking risks and stepping out in faith to see what God might do? That is the way you are going to find His anointing come upon you!

Since you are reading this book on healing, I assume that is what you are seeking today. If so, please read on.

Endnotes

[1] Acts 1:8

[2] Arndt, William et al. *A Greek-English lexicon of the New Testament and other early Christian literature* 2000: n. pag. Print.

[3] Joel 2:28-29

[4] Acts 2:1-4

[5] 1 Corinthians 12:1, 4-7

[6] Arndt; ibid

[7] Clark, Randy. *Ministry Team Training Manual.* Mechanicsburg, PA: Apostolic Network of Global Awakening 2004. Page 73.

[8] 1 Timothy 4:14

[9] 2 Timothy 1:6

[10] Romans 1:11

[11] Arndt; ibid

[12] Matthew 7:8-11

| 7 |

Gifts of Healing

In the last chapter, we discussed the "power gifts" of the Holy Spirit and how a person may receive one of those special anointings. Now, we will dig a little deeper into understanding the "gifts of healing," which is one of the nine anointings or "manifestations" of the Holy Spirit listed in 1 Corinthians 12:

> *"To each is given the manifestation of the Spirit for the common good. For to one is given through the Spirit the utterance of wisdom, and to another the utterance of knowledge according to the same Spirit, to another faith by the same Spirit, to another gifts of healing by the one Spirit, to another the working of miracles, to another prophecy, to another the ability to distinguish between spirits, to another various kinds of tongues, to another the interpretation of tongues. All these are empowered by one and the same Spirit, who apportions to each one individually as he wills."*[1]

Healing Gifts

To understand the healing anointing, we must see that a person does not receive "a gift of healing." Instead, the word for "gift" in Greek is plural. The anointing from God is for "gifts of healing."

This is an interesting distinction in how the gifting for healing has been viewed in the 20th century, where certain leaders claimed to carry the healing "gift" as though it is an official position. We have seen many famous evangelists take on the title of "divine healer" or "God's man of power." Unfortunately, there is not an office of healer in the New Testament.

There is Not an Office of Healer

The five spiritual "offices" given in the New Testament are apostles, prophets, evangelists, pastors, and teachers. This is often referred to as the fivefold ministry. The Bible says these are unique callings placed on certain people by Jesus Himself, rather than by the Holy Spirit as in 1 Corinthians.

> *"But grace was given to each one of us according to the measure of Christ's gift. Therefore it says, 'When he ascended on high he led a host of captives, and he gave gifts to men.'...And he gave the apostles, the prophets, the evangelists, the shepherds and teachers..."*[2]

These "offices" are directly tied to the long-term discipleship and empowerment of the church (see Ephesians 4:11-16). Therefore, they should be considered God-given job descriptions rather than hierarchical titles to go in front of our names on a business card.

Gifts vs. Offices

To better explain, let me divert from healing for a minute...

In the two scriptures quoted above, you may notice that there is a calling of "Prophet" given by Jesus in Ephesians, and there is also the gift of prophecy given by the Holy Spirit in 1 Corinthians. These two things are not the same!

When Paul writes about the gift of prophecy and its use in the church, he says, "you can all prophesy one by one" (1 Corinthians 14:31). The implication is that every member of the church can, at times, give prophetic utterances from the Lord. That is the gift of prophecy from the Spirit. This does not mean that all believers are Prophets by calling or office.

Those who operate in the office of Prophet have an assignment on their lives to lay the directional foundations of the church and nations (Ephesians 2:20). Their prophetic gift is constantly at work in Christ, and their revelation is often much deeper than an "occasional" gift of prophecy received when someone comes under the anointing.

The reason I divert to prophecy is that this distinction between giftings and offices is important in understanding how gifts of healing work. Contrary to prophecy, healing does NOT connect directly with a spiritual office given by Jesus. As I said before, there is not an office of healer in the Bible (remember, we all have authority to heal!).

This becomes foundational to understanding why Paul uses the plural "gifts" when discussing how the Holy Spirit brings His anointing for healing.

Various Types of Healings

As I have read the writings of various ministers, contemporary and historical, who are each recognized for their healing gifts, there are differing opinions for why the word "gifts" is plural.

One explanation is because there are various types of healing that a person can receive, such as:

- physical wounds like broken bones or open lesions
- bodily infirmities like HIV or diabetes
- mental illnesses like schizophrenia
- emotional illnesses like anxiety or depression
- soul-sicknesses, such as issues coming from traumatic experiences or abuse
- spiritual sickness, often coming from demonic strongholds and torments

Another explanation is that there are various means by which God brings healing, such as:

- the laying on of hands
- anointing with oil
- the word of command
- anointed items such as Paul's prayer cloths
- anointed presence such as Peter's shadow
- inspired human wisdom in medical professionals

Every Healing is Another Gift

While those explanations are merely speculation, there may be a lot of truth to them, and they do offer helpful observations in how we think about healing. Still, I prefer a much simpler explanation.

I believe that the reason Paul uses the plural "gifts" when discussing healing is that each healing that takes place is a distinct gift being given to the person healed.

That means that I, as the minister, do not receive the "gift of healing" as though it is an office. Instead, when operating in this anointing of the Holy Spirit, God uses me to deliver His gifts of healing to those in need. It is not my gift; it is God's gift being given *through* me to others.

If someone gets healed of cancer, that is their gift. If someone gets healed of three broken ribs, they have received three gifts of healing. Each sickness or condition God heals is another gift!

God's Delivery Person

What I like about this understanding is that it removes the pressure from me as the minister. I am not the one controlling the gift, and therefore do not have to feel the pressure to perform.

Instead, I simply act as the delivery man bringing God's gifts to people as He chooses to distribute them. It is His good pleasure and His timing, not mine! (Side note: this is why the gift of Words of Knowledge is often connected with healing. God shows His servant, in advance, the gift of healing He plans for them to deliver.)

When someone is healed of anything, we give God all the praise. When someone is not healed, we don't get discouraged but learn to press into Him more and more for His gifts!

Pursuing the Gift to Get the Anointing

As we said before, the gifts you receive will be determined largely by how you are pursuing God and how you are seeking to love others. God seems to give healing anointing to those who are praying for the sick. (And unless you pray for the sick, you cannot know if the anointing is there in the first place!)

If you want to learn to operate in your authority and receive God's anointing for healing, you have to step out and pray for the sick. That is where we will turn in our last chapter.

Endnotes

[1] 1 Corinthians 12:7-11

[2] Ephesians 4:7-8,11

| 8 |

How to Pray for the Sick

We have come a long way in this small book on Christian Healing! First, we began with the biblical basis for healing, then discussed if healing should be expected today. Next, we looked at the authority of all believers to heal the sick and talked practically about "healing by command." Then, shifting directions from authority to anointing, we looked at the Holy Spirit's power for healing, and in the last chapter, we discussed the biblical "gifts of healing."

Now, finally, with the foundations having been laid, I hope you are ready to go after healing and begin praying for the sick yourself!

In this chapter, I want to share the most effective prayer model for healing I have ever seen. It is the one I have used when praying for the sick for almost a decade, and it is the one we teach to all of our churches, team members, and ministry partners in our ministry in Africa.

Are Prayer Models Biblical?

Before I lay out the steps for praying for the sick, I first want to deal with the objection that prayer should be a spontaneous conversation with God rather than following a structured format.

I do agree with that sentiment completely. We should not be ritualistic in our relationship with the Lord. However, in the New Testament, as the disciples walked with Jesus and saw him doing public ministry, as well as observing His private life of prayer with the Father, they knew something was missing in their own prayer life. Based on what they saw, they asked Him, "teach us to pray," at which point Jesus gave them what we now call "The Lord's Prayer" or "The Model Prayer."

> *And he said to them, "When you pray, say:*
> *"Father, hallowed be your name.*
> *Your kingdom come.*
> *Give us each day our daily bread,*
> *and forgive us our sins,*
> *for we ourselves forgive everyone who is indebted to us.*
> *And lead us not into temptation."*[1]

This prayer was not intended to be used for repetitive, ritual recitations. Nor was it supposed to be a formula to get God to move on their behalf. It was simply given to them as a model to follow as they began to pray to the Lord for themselves.

In the same way, the prayer model I will share is not a "repeat these words" kind of prayer, nor is it a "principle" to get God to do what you want. Instead, it is a method of thinking about praying for the sick, enabling a person to minister effectively.

I learned this prayer model in 2012 from Dr. Randy Clark, and it has forever changed my fruitfulness in the healing ministry.[2]

How to Pray for the Sick

As you enter into a time of ministry with the sick, it is important to check your personal motivations first. Although we desire to see miraculous healing take place, our primary goal is that the person would experience the love of God working through us and personally connect with Jesus in the process. It is never our goal to glorify ourselves or to "show off" with God's power.

When Jesus healed the sick, He always did so out of compassion (see Matthew 14:14 and Mark 1:41). That must be our motivation as well.

Secondly, for healing to occur, we must be praying with faith that God wants to heal. We should never offer a quick prayer, saying, "God, if it is your will, please heal this person." That is not loving to the person, and it shows little faith.

Jesus never left a sick person in their illness, saying, "It isn't in the plan for you today." His will is to heal. We must believe that if we are to pray effectively.

Praying for the sick should be an earnest pursuit, seeking God to touch the individual and free them from the bondage of sickness and disease. This five-step prayer model will help you do that.

Step 1: Interview

When a person was brought to Jesus for healing, He usually took time to question them before jumping into prayer. His question, often, was *"What do you want me to do for you?"* (see Luke 18:41).

We, too, must take time to talk to the person needing healing to find out what is going on and how they want us to pray. Begin by asking questions like:

- How can I pray for you today?
- What sicknesses or injuries do you have?
- How long have you had this issue?
- On a scale of 1-10, where is your pain level to begin with? (This question will set a baseline for watching their improvement as you pray.)
- What is/was the cause?
- What are the doctors telling you about this condition?
- Do you take any medications for this?

Listen to Them

The basic goal of this step is to try and understand what they want prayer for. We must ensure our prayer is in line with their desires, not our own.

Recently I was leading a healing crusade in a rural district in Uganda. A man came forward for prayer, walking with a cane, and had one foot twisted sideways by polio. A chair was brought for him, and I automatically assumed that this was what he wanted prayer for, so I knelt beside him to place my hands on his leg. Thankfully, I caught myself, and as I knelt, I asked him, "How can I pray for you today." He told me that he has suffered greatly with constant ringing in his ears and was going deaf in one of them. He wanted me to pray for his hearing!

It took some time and multiple prayers, but we did see the man's hearing healed. Afterward, I asked if he wanted prayer for his twisted leg as well. Unfortunately, he wasn't interested at that time. The thing *I* wanted to pray for was not *his* priority.

At other times I have had people in wheelchairs only wanting prayer for back pain or stomach sicknesses. But, of course, I wouldn't have known that without asking them.

Listening to the person, rather than jumping to conclusions, is loving them. That is our first priority during any time of prayer!

Listen to the Holy Spirit

As much as you are listening to what the person has to say in the interview time, you should also be listening to the Holy Spirit for His insight into the problem. For instance, some sicknesses may have roots in spiritual issues such as sin, bitterness, unforgiveness, emotional wounds, or even the effects of a curse or a demonic affliction. The Lord may give you words of knowledge or words of wisdom in how to deal with these issues.

Keeping in tune with the Holy Spirit as we minister demonstrates that our faith for healing depends solely on Him and not our own wisdom or abilities.

Step 2: Prayer Selection

In the New Testament, we can see two different styles of prayer demonstrated by Jesus and His disciples when praying for the sick. The first is a petitioning prayer. This is when we ask the Lord to heal the person. For example, *"God, right now I ask in Jesus Name, that you would take this pain from my brother..."* (We see this type of prayer called for, in conjunction with the use of anointing oil, in James 5:14.)

If you are praying for someone with an unseen disease where immediate healing would not be detectable, such as cancer or diabetes, you might opt to pray with a petitioning prayer. Since there may be no physical manifestations taking place, and they likely would not know if they are healed immediately, there is no need to rush or continually stop and reinterview. Instead, your prayer time should be long enough that the person feels encouraged and loved through the time of ministry. Love them and let them know your faith is with them for their healing.

The second way we see Jesus and the disciples heal is by command (which we have already discussed, in-depth, in chapter 5). This is when, rather than petitioning God to do something, we speak to the disease or injury in the name of Jesus and command it to leave. For example, *"In the name of Jesus, I command this pain to go, now."* (We see this type of prayer demonstrated by Peter in Acts 3:6.)

Dr. Randy Clark says, *"A command is appropriate as your initial step unless you are led otherwise by the Holy Spirit..."*[3] This is especially true when there has been a word of knowledge given for their specific issue.

If you are praying for a very evident affliction like a crippled hand or a visible tumor, you should begin by praying with commanding prayer and watching for any change in the condition. Also, if you are praying for an unseen affliction, but where healing would be immediately evident to that person, such as back pain or TMJ (popping in the jaw), you would likely want to pray shorter prayers, using commands, and re-interview often to find out what they are feeling if anything.

You would also use a command when there is evidence of a demonic power causing the affliction or when breaking a curse over the person. For example, *"In Jesus' name, I break the curse over this person, and command this afflicting spirit to leave..."*

After you have interviewed the person and discerned what the Holy Spirit is saying, you should decide which prayer to begin your ministry time with. Don't worry about making a wrong choice, as you will likely be praying more than one time and can change your approach as the Spirit and situation lead you.

Step 3: Pray

This step is pretty straightforward. Pray for the person using the style of prayer you chose in step 2.

Some tips for praying:

Ask the person not to pray. Instead, they should be resting and positioned to receive from the Lord. Eyes closed and open hands held in front of them is appropriate. They should also be paying attention to their body for any changes in their condition or other manifestations of the Spirit.

Keep your eyes open during your prayer. Watch for any physical activity that may tell you if the Spirit is doing something.

Sometimes during prayer, people will feel extreme temperature changes, especially in the pray-er's hands. They may also be moved to laughing or crying. They may begin to shake. They may fall down. All of these have been viewed through Christian history as potential signs that God is working. Let it build your faith that God is touching them.

Always pray in Jesus' name. That is where our authority to heal lies. By praying in His name, we are speaking with the authority He gives to us as His church.

Even if you do not see immediate results, keep your love turned on and your faith in God high. Don't rush away too soon!

Step 4: Re-Interview

After praying for a short time, especially when commanding sicknesses to leave, you should stop often and re-interveiw that person. In this step, you are trying to discern, if possible, whether healing is occurring. You want to ask questions like, *"How is your pain level now?" "Are you feeling anything?" "Can you move it any more than before?"*

If it is a physical affliction where healing would be evident immediately, ask them to try and do something they couldn't do before. Of course, they should not be forced to do something that will injure them worse. However, sometimes the simple act of faith to attempt something they couldn't do before is the catalyst for their immediate healing.

It is important to understand that many times healing prayer is not met with immediate results. On the contrary, many modern-day ministers who operate in the healing gift consider instantaneous healing a "miracle" gift rather than a gift of healing.

This means that you might minister to one person for a good amount of time while seeing progressive healing take place a little more each time you pray. Be encouraged by this. It shows God is working through you! Jesus, Himself, prayed for one blind man multiple times before the man was healed (see Mark 8:22-25)!

Look for Hidden Causes

During the re-interviewing process, you may need to ask further questions, looking for a deeper cause for a stubborn illness where no healing is taking place. For instance, if the person was injured by another person years before, perhaps they need to forgive the person before healing comes actively. Unfortunately, people will not always be forthcoming with heart issues, so these things may take time to uncover. Also, remember to trust the Holy Spirit's guidance in this.

One other thing to be aware of is that the demonic can play a role in sickness without the person realizing it. This can become apparent when the infirmity increases in intensity or pain begins moving from one location in the body to another. When this is the case, you should begin praying to cast out the spirit (by command) rather than praying about the condition.

When to Stop Praying

After you re-interview them, return to steps 2 through 4 again, as necessary. You may pray and re-interview many times during one ministry session.

I once prayed for a woman with pain in her neck, shoulders, and upper back, which she had carried for a few years. She began by telling me her pain was a 9. After three prayers, it finally moved down to an 8. Then a 7. Then a 5. Then a 4.5 and a 4. All in all, I ministered to this lady for more than half an hour before the pain had completely left (as well as a spirit of affliction, which became evident during the prayer). She walked away totally healed. Though I was getting frustrated with the incremental healing, I just kept telling myself, *"Jesus prayed again, so can I."*

You should stop praying when:

- The person is completely healed.
- The Holy Spirit leads you to stop.
- There has been no further healing taking place for some time, and you don't feel led to pray any other way.
- The person asks you to stop.

Step 5: Give Follow-Up Suggestions

As you close out the time of ministry, there needs to be some resolution. Don't just walk away.

When A Person Is Healed:

If the person is healed, then all that is left to do is praise God together for this gift. Celebrate with that person, and reflect with them on God's faithfulness and love for them.

If the person who has been healed had to walk through the process of repentance of sin or forgiveness of a past wound in order to receive their healing, remind them that God has set them free from that as well. They no longer have the right to return to their bitterness or sin. To do so may, in fact, undo the healing they have just received.

Encourage the person to share their testimony of this experience. If possible, do so immediately in the meeting you are a part of, but if not, they should at least share with their family and friends what has taken place. In our ministry, we make it a priority to record video testimonies of every major healing which takes place, if at all possible. When we cannot get the recording, we will try to get the basics of the testimony in writing, so we can recall what God has done later.

When A Person Is Not Healed:

If the person is not healed, remember that we must leave them feeling loved by God and by us. Encourage them that sometimes healing is not immediate and may still come following this time of prayer.

For example, one of the pastors I trained in Uganda experienced a great disappointment during his first prayer time for healing. A lady came to the church with her child, who had a severe, terminal illness. As he prayed for the child, he was very nervous, so he recalled every scripture on healing he could think of to reassure himself, and prayed every way you can imagine. At the end of the session, the woman went home, very upset, with her still-sick child and the pastor walked away extremely discouraged. However, the next morning the mother returned to the church with a much different attitude because when she woke that day, her child was completely healed!

Remind the person you are ministering to that there are various reasons their healing might be delayed. They should keep waiting on the Lord and trusting in Him.

If the person is holding on to some sin, unforgiveness, or another issue that you feel is holding back their healing experience, then encourage them in the gospel and push them to seek repentance in that situation.

Whatever you do, never blame the person when they do not get healed. While it is true that sometimes a lack of faith is the reason we don't see healing occur, it is never our place to judge the level of faith in others. In fact, in Matthew 17, when the disciples were unable to heal an epileptic child, Jesus blames the disciples' lack of faith rather than that of the boy or his family.

Give them a scripture they can hold to, if one comes to mind, looking to the full promise of God for their life and eternity. Make sure you encourage them to keep praying and seeking God to grant them this miracle. And where possible, encourage them to seek prayer from others and continue to press into God in intimacy.

It's Your Time

I hope that through this chapter and all those leading up to it, you have had your biggest questions answered and that you are feeling more equipped to pray for the sick. My final word of advice is "try."

In my own journey into healing ministry (which you can fully read in the appendix), I was praying for people every week for months before God brought the breakthrough moment and people began getting healed. I prevailed by continuing to go after it.

After Heidi Baker, world-renown missionary in Mozambique, first received the Word of the Lord that she would see the blind see, the deaf hear, and the dead raised, she prayed for the blind and deaf in her area of Mozambique daily for over a year, before any of them began to be healed.

Before modern-day evangelist Todd White saw the healing breakthrough come, he had prayed for over 700 people to be healed!

This same story can be repeated endlessly, with various names of well-known ministers, and it might well prove to be the same with you.[4] You have to keep praying and believing!

As I mentioned before, I believe it was John Wimber who first said, "Faith is spelled R-I-S-K."[5] The only way you will begin to see people get healed is to step out in faith, take the risk and pray for them.

Now that you have finished this book, it's time to go and get started!

Endnotes

[1] Luke 11:2-4

[2] From what I understand, this prayer model did not originate with Dr. Clark, but that he learned it from the ministry of John Wimber, founder of the Vineyard Church movement.

[3] Clark, Randy. *Ministry Team Training Manual.* Mechanicsburg, PA: Apostolic Network of Global Awakening 2004. Page 57.

[4] A note to pastors: The church should be a safe place for people to try out their spiritual gifts, be able to fail and make mistakes without condemnation, and grow into all they are called to be in the Lord. It is your job to be equipping the saints to do the work of ministry (Ephesians 4:11-12). I highly encourage you that if you are functioning in the healing ministry, to also be equipping your church members to do the same.

[5] This quote is attributed to John Wimber.

APPENDIX: MY JOURNEY INTO HEALING MINISTRY

Anytime I talk about the practicals of healing ministry, I feel like it is good to give my own background in the healing ministry. Hopefully this will add some credibility to what I am teaching or, at least, show that some psychological tricks have not been used to brainwash me.

I am attaching this as an appendix rather than a regular chapter in this book because I don't want the book's main thrust to be experience-based. However, now that I have written the entire book sharing the scriptural foundations for Christian healing, I will use this space to share my personal journey into the healing ministry.

I am a fairly average Christian. Yes, I am a pastor and missionary and all of that, but when I compare myself to the great heroes of the faith, I am usually left feeling un-remarkable. (I don't recommend you compare yourself to anyone but Jesus, by the way. It works out better for you in the long run.) Never in my life could I have imagined that God would use me in the healing ministry one day. Now, however, it is one of the greatest joys of my life.

Coming to Faith

Growing up and finding my own faith in Jesus was a journey in itself. My parents had left the independent Baptist church when I was four. Later, when I had questions, all the different denominational beliefs from my extended family left me feeling more confused than before I had asked.

By the age of 16, I knew that my faith in Jesus was real and that I was saved. I had rejoined the church from my childhood. Beyond that, I had no intention of anything in ministry. My life's trajectory was Texas Christian University's "Ranch Management" program. I was going to be a full-time cowboy.

Although this is not the place for my full life story, it will suffice to say that my course changed around the age of 18 as I felt God redirecting my priorities and leading me into the ministry. So, instead of TCU, I enrolled in the fundamentalist Baptist college recommended by my pastor. It also happened to be the same school where many of my extended family members had also pursued ministry education since the 1920s. Frankly, it was also the only Bible college I knew of, making the decision fairly easy to make.

Unbelieving Bible College

While in that Bible college, my faith really began to be tested and challenged. My hopeful outlook of God's big plan for the world was turned upside down by legalist rules and a lot of hypocritical, self-righteous attitudes by some of the students and faculty. Not to mention their belief that the supernatural gifts of God ceased after the 12 apostles died.

At the same time, I began reading the book of Acts, not only as a historical record of the early church but also as a book that would either validate Christianity as real or force me to consider that this whole thing was a myth. So I began to pray for God to expand my experience to fit my convictions about the Bible, and after a few months of praying, I was baptized in the Holy Spirit of God, just as the Bible promised.

Surprisingly to me, not everything in my life changed at once. Although there was a new, revitalized spirit within me, and my optimism of the Christian faith had been renewed (and there was definitely fruit being produced in my life from this change), I was also faced with a growing amount of controversy and hostility from peers and the college faculty. Nevertheless, my hunger for the things of God continued to grow.

Healing Enters the Picture

Along with my pursuit of the baptism of the Holy Spirit, I also became hungry to see the power of God at work. It was around this time in my journey that divine healing entered the picture.

First, it came through stories from both my grandmothers. On my mom's side, my grandma, Brenda, has always been a charismatic believer. She has always prayed in tongues and believed in God for miracles. Yet, for most of my life, I ignored her stories and moved along with my life. (In the worst times, I argued with her from my Baptist education and hurt our relationship in many ways.) However, over a holiday break in college, she began recounting to me, again, all of the many miracles of healing she had seen over the years. Not only in her own body and in our family, but through former pastors and other believers she used to know. Though these stories were not new to me, I did pay more attention to them now.

It was my other grandma, Polly, who surprised me with her stories of healing, however. She had been raised in the Church of Christ her whole life until she married my granddad and moved over to the fundamental Baptist church where he was a member (and where I had also attended as a child and again from the age of 16).

This grandma began to tell me of different things she had seen in her own Christian life that her (our) church would not validate, yet she knew them to be true.

The craziest story she told me was a testimony from when she was young. She was diagnosed with a severe case of appendicitis which was nearing a rupture. The doctors told the family that there was nothing they could do medically and sent her home. It was her older sister, however, who refused to accept that answer. This older sister, who was a faithful member of the Church of Christ until the day she died, took my grandmother out to the barn, laid her down in some hay, laid hands on her, and prayed a prayer of faith. My grandma's pain instantly left, and soon everyone saw that she had been completely healed.

These stories from my own family – people I loved and trusted more than anyone – began to sink into me and stir up that hunger to see God move in these ways again.

More Stories of Healing Today

Following that Christmas break, my faith for healing went beyond accepting the stories of the past to being open for the present. This was largely due to my good friend Bobby returning to college with stories of his own.

While on break, he went back to see his family in Florida but soon found that circumstances with his parents were quite different than when he left. They had moved from their Baptist church and were now "spirit-filled," praying in tongues and attending a local Pentecostal congregation. The first week home, his parents asked Bobby, and his brother, who also attended college with us, to visit the church just once to see that their parents were not crazy.

Bobby came back with incredible stories of not only healing but mind-reading prophecies, as well. On the healing front, he had watched his grandfather's swollen ankle shrink back down to normal size through the pastor's prayer. His grandmother, who had been keeping her arm in a sling, was also prayed for and was able to lift her arm above her head with full strength.

One prophecy was made over his brother, that he would receive a healing anointing. That evening the pastor called him up to lay hands on an elderly woman being prayed for. The woman fell under God's power, and the pain in her back completely left. (She did end up with a minor headache, as she bumped her head on the pew as she went down...)

All of these stories, old and new, built a burning desire in me to see God's healing power for myself. It didn't take long.

I Got Healed

Back at Bible college, a few stagnant months went by until Bobby got invited to a "revival" meeting at the church of a Nigerian missionary to the U.S. We couldn't wait to go, based on the pastor's presentation of the revival as being full of "healings, miracles, deliverances, and more!"

However, on the first day of the revival meeting, I woke up in the morning in terrible pain. My stomach felt like something had ruptured inside, and I couldn't deal with it. I skipped class that day to go to the E.R, where I received x-rays and an MRI of my stomach, all to no avail. The diagnosis I left with was the same as I had written on my intake form: "extreme abdominal pain."

Discouraged and still hurting, I managed to go to the revival service that night, where we did, in fact, see many incredible things we had only imagined up to then. Demons were being cast out. People were falling under God's power (although, at the time, we still struggled to accept that as really being from God).

It was at the end of the night that the pastor said something like, "I know some of you came for healing, but we are not praying for the sick one-by-one tonight. We are doing that tomorrow. However, if you are sick, God can still heal you, now;" and he prayed a general prayer over the congregation.

To my surprise, as he prayed this prayer, all of the pain in my stomach instantly left. No trace. And it never came back!

As people were leaving, I went to greet the pastor and told him of my healing. He quickly put me on the mic to share with the dispersing crowd what God had just done to help raise their expectations for the next night. Needless to say, we made sure to go back!

Years of Charismatic Stagnation

Unfortunately, without a strong community of faith around me to encourage and guide me, my Christian walk remained rather stale from that time on. In addition, I was still in an *unbelieving* Bible college and struggling with the pessimistic Christian culture and the little bits of ongoing backlash I faced there. Nevertheless, I did graduate in 2007 with a Bachelor of Science degree in Biblical Studies.

Two years before, I had begun interning in the summers with a missionary group in Mexico, and I spent June of '07 with them near Saltillo. Immediately after that, I took my first trip to Uganda with my friend, Micah, in July.

On that trip, we again saw things that piqued our interest in spiritual, supernatural realities: deliverances taking place, healing evangelism at work, etc. Still, although I was built up in my faith, it didn't have any practical effect on actually bringing me into doing those things myself.

From there, I returned to west Texas and, through a friend's recommendation, joined the staff of Grace Baptist Church in Odessa as Associate Pastor. Shortly thereafter, I was also invited to minister with another international missionary organization on a volunteer basis, which took me back to East Africa multiple times, as well as India, Israel, and Haiti.

Again, I believed wholeheartedly in healing, and at times would try my hand at praying for the sick, but I never saw healing take place. So, despite my desire, I began to think this gift was not for me.

In 2012, the mission organization's work in Haiti required the long-term presence of the U.S. Team, and I resigned from the church, became a full-time missionary-evangelist, and moved to Haiti for almost a year. It was during this time that I got serious about praying for the sick.

Continual Failure

While living in Haiti, I primarily oversaw the orphanage work of the ministry. However, I was also preaching in church services every Sunday and often on other days as well. Within the church culture there, it is standard for people to approach the pastor for prayer following every service. As these poor people do not have the financial ability to visit doctors for general health issues, most of my praying each week centered on physical healing.

Sunday after Sunday, I prayed for neck pain, back problems, recurring headaches, arthritis, cold and flu-like symptoms (common to the people in the mountains where I was staying), and more. These weren't "major" healing issues like cancer or AIDS, so for some reason, my mind thought these things should be easier to see healed. They weren't.

It did not matter what I did. Week after week, no one was getting healed. Not once, from March to October, did a single person claim to be healed through my prayers. I didn't know what was happening. I had been reading every scripture about prayer. I believed that, as James says, the prayer of faith would heal the sick (see James 5:15). I was praying with all the faith I could manage yet was met with a continual failure to see healing manifest. I had no idea what was wrong.

My Introduction to Dr. Randy Clark

At this time, I began looking for mature Christian leaders who had verifiable healing ministries from whom I could learn.

I read a few biographies of different ministers in the past who had great healing ministries. They were faith-building, but they didn't teach me *how* to actually pray for the sick effectively. I watched some YouTube videos of modern street-evangelists who practiced healing, and I got a few insights from them. However, the turning point was when I found a book on the Apple Bookstore by two men named Randy Clark and Bill Johnson. The book was called "The Essential Guide to Healing."[1]

Even though these men were quite famous in charismatic circles already, I have to admit I did not know anything about them. Quite honestly, had I known beforehand that Randy was involved with that "Toronto Blessing" some Baptist pastors had warned us about back in Bible College, I probably wouldn't have read the book at all.

However, as I began the book and read their biographical stories in the first two chapters, much of the spiritual life of Randy resonated with my own upbringing – charismatic grandparents, faith-filled youth, Baptist education that challenged it all, and a lot more. I immediately knew this was someone I would learn from.

As I continued the book, I learned Randy's "five-step prayer model" for healing (the same one I shared in chapter 8), and I began using it in my post-church service prayers. Still, nothing happened...

I also read in the book about "impartation," or the transferring of anointing through the laying on of hands, and I began to think that perhaps this is what I needed. After all, I had never been part of a charismatic church. Nor had I ever really been mentored by anyone in the ministry beyond what classroom lectures could teach. I had certainly not been prayed for in this way before.

I began to question my own assumptions, which I had held for years, that you either have a gift or you don't, and that they would simply appear one day and just work if that was God's will for you. (While that may be true at times, what I have found is that most of the time, spiritual gifts are not instant.)

It began to make more sense to me that the charismatic gifts of the Holy Spirit would likely be learned, built upon, and passed through the Christian community, from one generation to another, just as they did in the Bible. They are meant to be developed in a person as part of their life in the body of Christ.

Promise of Impartation

One night, as I was sitting on the rooftop of the house where I lived in Haiti, I prayed and asked God to speak to me about healing and growing in the gift. Finally, after what felt like hours, I very clearly heard Him speaking to me, saying, "In October, Randy will be doing a conference. If you go to the conference, he will lay hands on you, and you will receive an impartation for healing."

I got so excited. I didn't even know Randy Clark would consider coming to Haiti, so I quickly began to look at his website to find out when he would visit!

Unfortunately, I discovered that he was not coming anywhere near Haiti.

Instead, what I learned was that at the end of October, Randy would be hosting his biggest conference of the year in Lancaster, Pennsylvania, called "The Voice of the Apostles."[2] This potentially life-changing conference just happened to be taking place a few days before I was supposed to go to South Sudan with my organization. I immediately began making arrangements to go.

Confronting My Doubts

During the conference, as I once again came into a major charismatic event as an outsider, I began to see and experience things I could never imagine. I questioned many things happening around me, and thankfully, was given quick validation from the Lord almost every time that what I was seeing was from Him.

There was holy laughter taking place through Rolland Baker of Iris Ministries, which I strongly doubted was real until I was the one on the floor laughing.

There were angelic encounters! I had been feeling a slight tickle on the top of my head for three days when, finally, a woman came to me and asked, "Do you know you have an angel messing with your head? I have seen him from across the room for three days but was never close enough to you to tell you." Unfortunately, she wasn't sure what he was doing. (I can tell you that the whole event did mess with my mindset about God and His work, though...)

There were words of knowledge for healing coming from many of the speakers. But, again, I was skeptical until Georgian Banov called out "old knee injuries from basketball accidents." This was for me! I had received terrible knee injuries in 8th-grade basketball and actually had to quit sports because of it. As I went forward for prayer, I was instantly healed, again!

Impartation

Finally, the time came for Randy's impartation session. As over 8,000 people were praying for the touch of God on their life, I was beginning to get discouraged that my impartation might not actually come as the Lord had told me.

As Randy led us into this time, he said, *"There is no way I can pray for all of you, but I have a team here who have traveled with me around the world. If you begin to sense God touching you – if you feel electricity in your body or heat, or you get cold, or if you begin to shake – then put your hand in the air, and my team will come to you to pray."*

As Randy prayed over the room, I told the Lord, *"You said Randy would pray for me, but if it comes through his team, I will take whatever You have for me here."* At that, my right hand began to shake uncontrollably.

After his prayer, Randy left the platform, and I began to put my shaking hand in the air to receive prayer from the team. Quickly, however, Randy turned back to the microphone and said, *"I forgot to say it, but if you are a full-time missionary or evangelist, come up here on stage. I want to pray for you."*

As quickly as I could get there, I climbed onto the stage. I was the second person in line when Randy began to pray for us. All I remember was him putting his finger on my open hands in front of me and saying, "Lord, I bless what You are doing in Anthony..." (which he read on my nametag), and I fell to the floor under God's presence.

Two hours later, Randy's stage crew came to clear our incapacitated bodies from the stage for the next session's soundcheck. I stumbled back to my chair, still feeling the weightiness of God's presence, where I sat with an electric pulse occasionally hitting my body and causing me to jerk and twitch. (This lasted for over a week, causing my dad, a long-time paramedic, to wonder what was wrong with his son. He thought I might have had a stroke or was having micro-seizures.)

Something had definitely happened in Randy's prayer, though. Could this be what I had been seeking for years? Could this actually be an impartation for healing? I supposed time would tell.

To South Sudan

After Randy prayed for me at Voice of the Apostles in 2012, and the conference ended, I went and saw my family for a few days before getting on a plane to fly to South Sudan.

This trip was the most extreme and difficult mission I had ever taken part in up to that point. Our host told us that our previous trips in Uganda would look like life in America compared to what we would face in the remote, tribal area we were now working in.

To get there, we flew from the U.S. to Nairobi, Kenya, then took a tiny plane to Lokichoggio, Kenya, in the north. (Each person was only allowed 15 pounds of luggage, including carry-on!) Arriving at that small airport, we were told it should take an hour to reach the border, and less than 1.5 hours, total, to get to the village of Narus, our final destination. However, as we waited for a few hours for our drivers to arrive, we began to figure out that something was wrong.

We soon learned that it had poured rain all night, causing the vehicles coming to get us to be delayed. Then for the next six mud-soaked hours, we crawled toward the border crossing in our struggling, little hatchback cars. Arriving there, we were forced to abandon the vehicles and wade across the flooded riverbed that marks the Kenya-South Sudan border carrying our luggage on our heads, then deal with an immigration officer who was angry about having to work so late in the day waiting for our team to arrive. This was just the start of a rough trip.

From there, the next couple of days were marked by team members freaking out over a lack of plumbing, bats circling overhead in their rooms, and rats coming out of the mattresses while some of our ladies slept. Finally, after resolving that we knew God had called us there and we were not turning around and going home, our team organized ourselves for a morning of prayer and worship. From that moment on, everything changed.

My Healing Breakthrough

After praying for the sick regularly for over a year, it was on our third day in South Sudan where my healing breakthrough finally came. As our team ventured out to see the mango tree where our host church gathered, most of the team members were talking to some tribal Taposa women who had come around to see "the whites."

My attention, however, was drawn to an old man, sitting alone, at the base of the giant mango tree. When I got close to him, I could see that all the color in his eyes had gone and that he was completely blind. (I would find out from his family on my return trip the following year that he went blind from alcohol poisoning after a lifetime of drinking almost a gallon of the local brew each day.)

Suddenly I was overcome by the Lord's love for this man. I collapsed in the dirt beside him and laid hands on him, and began to pray.

I have no idea exactly what I was saying in this prayer. For the first time, I was being led in healing prayer by the Spirit alone and prayed in faith, absolutely believing something was going to happen. After a few minutes, one of our Ugandan pastors came and began praying with me. Slowly, over the next 20 minutes or so, we began to watch the color come back to his eyes. As the team gathered around to see what was happening, it was obvious that his sight was getting better.

When we first began to pray, all he could see was the difference between light and dark – the same way we can see light and dark if we close our eyes and look toward the sun. As we prayed, he began to say things like, "I can see the green on the trees." "I can see the brown from the dirt." We kept praying. He began to say, "That one is a black man. That one is a white woman." It was obvious to all that God was working a miracle as we slowly watched the color return to his eyes.

Unfortunately, we couldn't remain there all day. Arrangements had been made for us to make our way to visit a hospital or prison or something. The trip kind of blurs in my mind now. As we left him, however, I knew the man was going to be completely healed.

It didn't take long for our hopes to be confirmed. At the end of the day, as our team met for supper back at our base camp, one of the local pastors we were working with came running into the dining room, very excited. "Pastor Scott, the blind man you prayed for is completely healed. He is walking around the village by himself with no one leading him! Everyone is talking about this miracle."

We found out that this man's adult children would bring him to the "church" tree each morning and leave him sitting in the shade with his jug in hand. They would bring him lunch there at some point, then come back in the evening to collect him and take him home. Now that he was walking around without being led, it was sure to capture people's attention!

Healing Evangelism

This whole trip was loosely planned as you never know how things will go in the bush of Africa. The next morning, very early on, we sent a local pastor to a village just over an hour away, where we were told the gospel had never been preached, to ask if we could bring our team and share with the people. The response of the village chief left us amazed at God's goodness.

He told our pastor that he had been approached by many missionaries over the years but had never allowed them to come to his village. He didn't want their stories. However, he then said, *"...but I have heard about the blind man, and we want those people to come here."*

A couple of hours later, we gathered our team into the cars and were on our way. We didn't have a sound system or any cool media technology. It was just our small group of believers, bibles in hand, off to see what God would do.

Once in this unreached village, I was given the privilege of sharing the Gospel with around 40 people who had gathered to hear what we had to say. My first question was, "How many of you are Christian?" All of them put their hand in the air. I was perplexed, but I quickly realized my mistake. This was South Sudan. Politically speaking, Northern Sudan was Muslim, but Southern was "Christian" in the old, Catholic-empire sense of the word.

My question that followed, then, was, "How many of you have ever heard of a man named Jesus Christ." This time, none of the locals raised their hand.

I began to share from the Bible on who Jesus was, why He came, and how each person can be saved. I told them of how Jesus had worked in his lifetime to get this message to the world, then continued through the early disciples and now the church. There was quite a bit of excitement when I gave the invitation, as all 40 people raised their hands to get saved by Jesus!

Afterward, I couldn't help myself. I began sharing how we had been praying for people all over Narus, our village base of operations, for various issues, from wanting to be pregnant to finding work. Then I shared the story of the blind man and told them, "We want to pray for you too."

We decided it was wise to have men pray with men and women with women due to some cultural sensitivities we had discovered the day before when one of our female team members accidentally "claimed" a Taposa warrior as a husband. Let's just say the rage of this man's wife would have been deadly, except for the quick response of our interpreter.

As eager as the men were to be prayed for, none of them came to me at first. Instead, they were waiting in respect as one of the oldest village elders came to receive prayer first.

This elderly man walked with the help of a stick and was very slow. A 10-meter walk took 2-3 minutes for him, unassisted. I patiently waited, out of respect, for him to reach me. He told me how his knees had been very damaged in the fight for independence and other tribal wars in the past and asked me to pray.

At the time, I was praying alongside another gentleman – a very devout leader in a cessationist Baptist church. He was already skeptical of the blind man's healing, wanting to know if we could verify he was actually blind before we met him; ignoring the fact that we personally watched the color return to his eyes. Let's just say he wasn't too enthused to be praying for healing with me, now, as his theology was getting in the way.

I placed my hands on the old warrior's right knee while my doubting companion grabbed the left. I prayed. As soon as I finished, the old man tested out his legs, and... nothing.

There was no change to his condition, and he thought that I didn't understand the problem correctly. I assured him I understood the need and shared with him (and my colleague) the passage where even Jesus had to pray for someone twice (see Mark 8:25). I said, "let's pray again." (This received a frustrated glance from my prayer partner, but he relented and grabbed the knee again.)

This time, as soon as we finished praying for his knees, I asked the man to test them out. He took one step, then took off running around the village center completely healed! I was so excited; I was shouting more than he was — my prayer partner, not so much.

More Healings

The next man to come forward was another warrior with the same issues, and the pattern followed the same. We prayed once, nothing happened. So we prayed a second time, and he ran around completely healed.

The third man had major back pain and was unable to lift or work easily. After a couple of prayers, the pain in his back completely left. At this point, so did my prayer partner. These healings were challenging his beliefs (or lack thereof) to the point that he went to pray with someone else.

The fourth man was different. He, too, was walking with a stick due to worn-out knees. I prayed for him once, but by this point, his faith was high after seeing all the other healings that he didn't check himself before taking off running. He ran. But

He wasn't healed! As he reached the edge of the village center, he collapsed in more pain.

The thing you need to understand about this situation is that these people are from a warrior tribe. Every man carries an 8-foot spear and can be very aggressive. They also value their elders. Now we had broken one of them.

As everyone's attention turned to the elder who had collapsed, out of fear for what might happen next, I took off running to the man, praying, "God, we broke him worse. They're going to kill us. Please, You have to heal Him now!"

As I reached the man, I immediately began praying for him again. This time, he listened when I asked him to test it out first, and praise God, he was completely healed.

Church Planting Made Simple

About this time, the chief, who had unfortunately missed our meeting due to other commitments, returned and began asking his people what was going on. All of the testimonies of how God was moving in salvation and healing through our team overwhelmed him. He immediately asked us to take up a permanent place in their village. They led us to the edge of town, where they donated a large plot of land to build a church and anything else we wanted to do (hospital, orphanage, etc.).

They pleaded with us to stay because, in their limited understanding of what had happened, they thought this power was coming from us rather than God's Spirit in us. They went as far as to ask if we could leave some of our women so that they could "mingle the blood" and receive this power. We explained to them that the power was not in us but in Jesus Christ through God's Spirit and that He would do these things through them if they learn to follow and obey him. We promised them that our local pastors would begin coming to work with them regularly in discipleship, then quickly left for the protection and comfort of some of our team.

I can happily report that today, 9 years later, there is still a growing church in that village led by the pastors who took us there in the first place.

I can also happily say that the senior pastor who hosted us on that first trip, a Ugandan missionary to South Sudan, became a good friend of mine and has since begun transitioning out of South Sudan (leaving the ministry there in the hands of the other pastors on his team). He is now planting a church in Busia, Uganda, under the covering of Sozo Ministries, the ministry God led me to open in 2015.

Ministering Through Words of Knowledge

It is difficult for me to share how much the healing ministry has shaped my work for the Lord in the years since this first breakthrough. Immediately following this trip to South Sudan, I returned to Haiti, where healing began happening every week during church services.

As I returned to the U.S. at the end of 2012, it felt like my opportunities to pray for people were becoming less and less. Deciding I needed to grow in my understanding of this gifting and have accountability to press in for more, I signed up for Randy Clark's online healing school[3], which pushed me to continue praying for the sick and growing in the gift. (I am now a member of Global Awakening's Association of Healing Ministers, and in 2019 I was ordained by Global Awakening — Dr. Randy Clark's Ministry — in the U.S.)

Through this program, I learned how to receive words of knowledge for healing, which has become one of the primary ways I minister in healing (and more).

In 2013, I left Haiti and returned to traveling around the world with the missionary organization I worked for, with shorter visits to Uganda, Kenya, South Sudan, India, Haiti, and Israel. Little by little, the gift continued to grow.

On a 9-day trip to India in 2014, the host pastors planned a crazy preaching schedule for me. We did 2 half-day pastor's conferences, one open-air crusade, and preached in 17 churches around the countryside. Not having time to prepare for each meeting beforehand, I really began to depend on words of knowledge to minister effectively. I would spend time praying in the car, on our way to each church, asking God to show me what to speak and what He wanted me to do.

Inevitably He would speak to me about scriptures I was supposed to share and show me pictures in my mind of how He wanted me to pray and minister to people. Surprisingly, praying for the sick became a large part of what He was showing me to do. In one church, He told me beforehand that every person with back pain would be healed. (They were.)

On that one trip to India, I saw more healings in 9 days than I had seen combined since South Sudan two years prior. As is sadly often the case, the supernatural work of the Holy Spirit brought in controversy among friends. Unfortunately, this large number of healings led to some challenges within the organization I was working for. As an interdenominational ministry, it was clear that not everyone in leadership believed the same things about healing that I did. The Lord led me to really check my motives, make sure this calling was from God, and see where He would take me next.

A New Ministry

The month before my trip to India, as a part of Randy's online healing school, I had been invited to attend a gathering of the International Society of Deliverance Ministers. There, I received two prophecies that would shape the current era of my life. One prophecy was a confirmation of my calling and directly concerned a shift in my ministry coming "very soon." The other was about God having "all the funding" ready for my "new ministry."

At the time, I held those prophecies loosely, until the following March, when, in a season of prayer and by mutual agreement with the leadership, I resigned from the missionary organization I worked with. (To be clear, this was not a divisive and angry split. Both sides felt like it was God's timing, and I remain friends with everyone in that organization today!)

Immediately I began work on registering Sozo Ministries, Inc.[4] with the state of Texas and working on non-profit status. We took the name "Sozo" because it is the Greek word for "saved" or "salvation" in the New Testament. However, if you look it up in a concordance, it means complete salvation – body, soul, and spirit – meaning that in Christ's atonement are the promises of salvation from sin, physical healing, and spiritual deliverance from the devil.

Since the foundation of Sozo Ministries in 2015, we have seen over 2000 people healed from various physical diseases and afflictions, in addition to thousands of salvations and hundreds of deliverances from demonic torments.

My Healing Ministry Today

As I now live in Uganda with my family and lead over 30 churches registered under Sozo Ministries in Uganda and Kenya, it is amazing to look back and see this journey the Lord has brought me on.

Today, I spend my time not only preaching the gospel and praying for the sick but training other pastors and believers to do the same.

Throughout the year, I preach in churches around East Africa (and in other countries as God opens the doors) and see healing happen in every single service. Sozo pastors plan gospel crusades throughout the year, and alongside them, I have the privilege of preaching to the lost, and again, in every meeting, people are getting saved and healed.

The largest event I am honored to be part of is the annual Global Outreach mission, in partnership with Living Water Ministries, Uganda[5], which takes teams of around 300 people on 2-3 week city-wide gospel outreaches. It is my privilege to help train the outreach team in healing and deliverance ministry and to lead the healing session at each mega crusade. Our last mission team saw over 600 healings during the three-week outreach. Less than 100 were through my prayers. It came through those who had been trained in our meetings and left equipped and filled with faith!

All in all, I can say that being a part of what the Lord is doing in saving the lost and healing the sick around the world is one of the greatest privileges of my life. Looking back at the 16-year-old me, I could never have imagined things going in this direction, but I wouldn't trade them for anything.

To be truthful, in many ways, I feel like my healing journey is still just beginning. Randy's impartation service and my healing breakthrough were only 9 years ago! I cannot wait to see what the next few decades have in store.

It's Your Turn

Hopefully, sharing my journey into healing ministry has encouraged you to pursue God for more in your own life. The Bible encourages us to pursue spiritual gifts (1 Corinthians 14:1) and seems to imply in many places that you will receive the gifts you ask for. So go after Him for more!

I would also ask you to pray for me. While I am confident that God heals — and see him do so often — I know there is more. I also know the challenges that come from both believers and nonbelievers concerning healing, and I need the boldness to remain faithful to God's calling.

Endnotes

[1] Bill Johnson and Randy Clark. *The Essential Guide to Healing: Equipping All Christians to Pray for the Sick* (Bloomington, MN: Chosen Books, 2011)

[2] www.VoiceOfTheApostles.com.

[3] www.HealingCertification.com

[4] www.SozoMinistries.net

[5] www.LivingWaterUganda.com

HOW TO CONNECT

You can follow my blog at www.AnthonyIngram.com or on most social media platforms under the username @IngramWriter, including Facebook, Instagram, LinkedIn, YouTube.

If your church or ministry is wanting to learn more about operating in the healing gift or wants to plan a gospel-healing outreach, it would be my pleasure to be invited to speak, or to offer guidance to your team in any way possible. You can email me directly at Scott@SozoMinistries.net.

You can keep up with my missionary work and our organization in East Africa at www.SozoMinistries.net. Be sure to check out our upcoming ministry trips there, if you're interested in joining a mission team to East Africa.

If you would like to support my family's missionary work financially (tax-deductible in the U.S.), you can do so at bit.ly/IngramSupport.

Finally, please be sure to send me your testimonies. I would love to hear how this book has encouraged your faith, and all the healings the Lord provides through your ministry. You can email them to blog@anthonyingram.com.

About The Author

Anthony Scott Ingram is the founder and apostolic overseer of Sozo Ministries International, a church planting and leadership training ministry working in the USA, Uganda, and Kenya. He currently lives in Mbale, Uganda with his wife, Liz, and their three children, Marley, Harper, and Liam.

Scott holds a Bachelor of Science degree in Biblical Studies from Arlington Baptist College, Arlington, Texas. He is ordained by the Apostolic Network of Global Awakening, and is also a member of Global Awakening's Association of Healing Ministers.

You can find out more about Scott at www.AnthonyIngram.com. You can find out more about Sozo Ministries at www.SozoMinistries.net.

Printed in the USA
CPSIA information can be obtained
at www.ICGtesting.com
CBHW072332210624
10451CB00044B/1302